The Cost of the
Anointing

Dr. Mia Y. Merritt

Copyright ©2013
THE COST OF THE ANOINTING
by
Mia Y. Merritt, Ed.D

All rights reserved. No part of this book may be reproduced in any form without permission in writing from the author or publisher.

ISBN # 978-0-9835830-8-0

Other Books by Mia Y. Merritt:
Prosperity is Your Birthright!
Prosperity is Your Birthright Workbook
Destined for Great Things!
Destined for Great Things Workbook
Words of Inspiration: Golden Nuggets for the Wise at Heart
Road to Inner Joy & Peace
Releasing Emotional Baggage
Money & How it Multiplies
Money & How it Multiplies Workbook
Life After High School
Life After High School Workbook
All About the Military
The Cost of the Anointing Workbook

Library of Congress Cataloging
in-Publication Data

Merritt, Mia

First Printing 2013
Printed in the U.S.A.

DEDICATION

This book is dedicated to my brothers and sisters in Christ who have a hunger and thirst for the truths of God and desire a closer walk with Him. The Christian walk is a faith walk and there are many twists and turns along the way. Salvation is free, but the anointing costs and the price is high! If you are willing to pay the price for the anointing, the reward is great. However, the tests, trials and struggles that you must endure to earn the anointing are not easy. The furnace is hot, the wilderness is lonely and the tribulations are discouraging. But God is faithful. He will not allow you to suffer more than you can handle. There is nothing that enters your life that God has not equipped you to be able to overcome. The rewards of this life come to those who do not crumble in the face of adversity. There is a reward that waits for the strong in Christ. Only the strong survive!

Bishop Dennis Jackson, thank you for being the father I never had. I appreciate your spiritual guidance and love. Through your wisdom, you discern when I'm fragile and you step in with your soothing fatherly prayers and words of encouragement. Words cannot express my gratitude.

Lavonia Waters, you have been a true friend, spiritual mother and big sister. Your wisdom, prayers and guidance have strengthened me many times over. I appreciate you and I am thankful that we are friends.

To my teenage son Stephan, my mother, my sisters and my true friends, thank you for your love and constant support. Without you, I would not be who I am today.

My daughter Stephanie,

Had you remained on earth, you would be 15 years old as of this writing. Please know that you are never forgotten. Your memory has remained alive in my heart and was birthed in your baby brother's heart the day he learned of you. He has embraced your spirit which has been imparted into Him and he speaks of you often. He sings to you on your birthday and draws you birthday cards; he buys you Christmas gifts and cries on the anniversary of your departure. You are loved by those you left on earth, but the love that your Heavenly Father has for you is far greater. I will see you again one day and we will all be reunited for eternity. Until then, continue to rest in peace.

Forever in my Heart,

~Mommy

TABLE OF CONTENTS

Introduction vii

Dedication iii

Chapter 1: In the Will of God 1

Chapter 2: The Fullness of Time 15

Chapter 3: Stepping Into Destiny 31

Chapter 4: Spiritual Gifts 47

Chapter 5: The Prosperity Anointing 65

Chapter 6: Amazing Grace 89

Chapter 7: Holding on to His Promises......................... 107

Chapter 8: Victory in Christ... 121

Epilogue 139

About the Author 140

Introduction

The origin of the word "anointing" came from a practice used by shepherds. Lice and other insects would often get into the wool of sheep, and when they got near the sheep's head, they could conceal themselves into the sheep's ears and kill the sheep; so the shepherds began pouring oil on the sheep's head. This made the wool slippery, which made it impossible for insects to get near the sheep's ears because they would just slide off. From this, anointing became symbolic of blessing, protection, and empowerment. Another definition of the word anointing means, "The presence and power of God". The title of this book encompasses all of the above definitions and the content of the book will outline the price that believers pay for the anointing. There are no shortcuts to the anointing. Salvation is free, but the anointing is costly and the cost for it is high! Through overcoming trials and tribulations by faith and trust in God, we earn the precious gift and power of the anointing. With this, also comes the weight of God's glory that rests upon the one who has endured and humbled themselves before God.

The number eight symbolizes "New Beginnings." This book intentionally has eight chapters because in spite of where you are right now, you are entering a realm of *New Beginnings.* God has ordained that you read 'The Cost of the Anointing' at this time because your mind, your spirit and your position in Christ are entering a new realm of anointed power. This book was written for those who earnestly desire to be elevated by God in this present day. It outlines powerful truths that the children of God may embrace to increase their faith in the promises of God. He has given us many gifts and weapons to assist in this Spiritual fight. However, many do not realize just how powerfully equipped they are and therefore do not use the power they have within. You are more than a conqueror through Christ Jesus, but if you sit on your power, do not make use of your weapons, and allow Satan to overtake you by killing your spirits, stealing your joy and destroying your hope, then your power is futile, ineffective, and useless. In order to fight this battle and win, you must be bold, diligent, wise, and confident in Him. This book will enlighten you to understand just how much power you have in Christ and will show you how to continuously and persistently use that power.

The Christian life should be a disciplined life and there are no shortcuts to anointed ministry. The righteous will be placed in the furnace of affliction so that they may be purified. The fire is hot. It burns and is painful, but is necessary for purification, learning, and elevation. As children of God, we must feed our Spirits more than we feed our flesh. As believers of Christ, God has called us out of the world, to be separated from the world and to become spiritually elevated in Him. When we become lovers of the world, conformers to the world, lovers of pleasure and aspirers after respectability, we are worldly-minded; but God has called us to be spiritually minded. Man was made from the dust of the ground and as we continue to feed the flesh, Satan feeds off of our carnal nature. When God passed the curse upon the serpent, his punishment was that he would eat the dust, signifying that he was to feed off of the carnal nature of man. In order to become elevated spiritually, we must feed our spirits through prayer, diligent study of the Word and earnest fasting. When the spirit is fed, the flesh becomes less powerful.

~Dr. Mia Y. Merritt

Chapter 1
In The Will of God

> *Enter ye in at the strait gate: for wide is the gate, and broad is the way, that leads to destruction, and many there be which go in thereat. Because strait is the gate, and narrow is the way, which leads unto life, few there be that find it.*
>
> *(Mathew 7:13-14)*

The safest place to be is in the will of God. God has a specific and detailed plan for your life and it is His utmost desire that the plan for your life be fulfilled. Many do not know God's will for their lives because they do not study His Word. Earnest study of the Word will reveal God's plan for your life. Not only do the sacred scriptures open up the plan of salvation for mankind, but it also reveals the plan that God has detailed concerning every aspect of your life. Every person in this universe was sent here with two things: a gift on the inside of them and an assignment to be achieved while on earth. It is sometimes not until puberty comes that people begin discovering their gifts. There are however, many whose gifts are so profound that they are identified in childhood. In those cases, there is no question about what their innate gift is. It is the will of God that we use our God-given gifts to bring glory to Him. Unfortunately, after many people identify their gifts, they use them for the world's benefit instead of using them to glorify God. At judgment, the use made of every talent will be scrutinized. Have we enhanced the powers entrusted to us in hand and heart and brain, to the glory of God and the blessing of the world? How have we used our time, our pen, our voice, our money, our influence rightly? What have we done for Christ in the person of the poor, the sick, the orphan, or the widow? God has given us gifts for a reason and He is looking for a return on His investment.

There is a difference between being gifted and being anointed. Your gift is the innate ability that you have for a skill that the average person does not have. Everyone has an innate gift. They do it with ease, love it, and with cultivation, become extraordinary at it. The "anointing" is the supernatural presence and power of God that rests upon a child of God. It is pronounced when you are flowing in His Spirit. Just because one is exceptionally gifted does not mean that they are anointed, but when you are BOTH gifted AND anointed, you have a power that can shake the world! The gift and assignment that God has given you are in line with His will for your life. Everything in this world is interconnected. Everyone has a predestinated path that leads to the unfolding of their destiny. God places each of our individual paths before us, but it is up to us to choose the path that He has marked. He never forces the will or the conscience. He does not force us to choose the right path because we have free-will and self-choice, but He does give us promptings and nudges through His Holy Spirit to choose right. He presents the choices to us, but it is up to us to make the right choices. He prepares the table before us, but it is up to us what to put on our plates. He shows us the direction in which to go, but it is up to us to walk it. There is always more than one path presented before us along this journey, but there is only one that is marked specifically for each person to take; and that "one" is the distinct path that leads to eternal life in heaven and peace and prosperity on earth. When we choose to take the wider more traveled road, we at some point will end up at a dead end. Misery, trouble, disappointments and problems are found on the wider more traveled road, although it looks appealing at first. The broader, more traveled path leads to destruction. When the narrow path is chosen, it leads to peace, joy, prosperity, and eternal life, but the narrow path requires self-discipline. The Christian's life should be a disciplined life. That is why we are called "disciples" which means "disciplined one." The road to eternal life is a narrow and difficult path. There are no shortcuts. The straight and narrow path appears hard to walk at first, and is not appealing, but the reward waits for those who will take it. Unfortunately, there are only a few who willingly choose to take that straight and narrow road. In their minds, they want freedom, but what appears to be freedom at first actually leads to bondage and what appears to be bondage at first is actually what sets us free.

CHOOSING THE RIGHT PATH

During our lifetime, we will evolve into different directions. Although we may start off together, at some point, we will begin diverging into different directions. No two paths are the same for any two people. You cannot go where God has predestined someone else to go no matter how bad you may want to. You have your own path to travel and you must travel it. You can take the direct route (straight and narrow) or the scenic route (wide and broad) to get to your destiny. Ideally, the way in which we evolve should lead to the path where we find our destiny, but we sometimes veer off onto an unmarked path that leads to a dead end. When this happens, we must detour our way back to the starting place and choose another path. It is not until we get to a major crossroad that we begin to wonder, *"What is the purpose for my life?"* It is at this juncture that we begin seeking the Lord for answers. It is God's desire that we know what His plans are for us. He takes no pleasure in having us ignorant of His purpose for our lives. However, He wants us to *seek* Him *diligently* for answers. We must seek Him as a lost and valuable treasure; and He does not make knowing His will, His plans and His secrets easy. If they were attained too easily, we would not appreciate them. He wants you to seek Him earnestly for the answers you desire. He is like the father who teaches his toddler to walk by backing away so that the child will have to take more steps to reach him. Eventually, the toddler takes enough steps that satisfy the father and he allows the baby to finally reach him with open arms. Getting clarity on God's will for your life requires a personal, intimate relationship with Him by seeking Him.

Too many Christians have religion, but not relationship. You must have one-to-one frequent communication time with the Lord. He has to be YOUR God, not your mother or father's God, not your pastor's God, but YOUR God. Jesus is the cornerstone of all creation. He is the only foundation for human life. When we come to truly know Him and not just "about" Him, changes in our personalities will no longer come from externals. They will only come from what is on the inside. His perfect love casts out all fear. In Him, we do not live by fear, but by faith. Your relationship with Him must go beyond the pastor and anything else that you have heard or read. You must know Him for yourself. He should not be the God of your grandparents or forefathers or the God of Bible stories to you. He must be the God that you know for yourself. Your relationship with Him must be real and true, alive and active, constant and consistent. Your relationship must consist of prayer, praise, worship and study of the sacred scriptures. The closer you get to Him through the application of these practices, the clearer His will for your life will be. He will navigate circumstances that will direct you to where you need to be in order to manifest your greatest potential. Experiencing God is spiritual and comes only when you transcend your human mind. God cannot be understood fully by human reasoning because human reasoning is of the flesh, and the

Spirit and the flesh do not agree. Being in the will of God does not mean that things will always be great. There are some disappointments and pitfalls along the way even in His will, but as long as you are in His will, things will always work together for your good. Being in God's will does not necessarily mean that you are in His perfect will either. Understand that there is the *perfect* will of God and the *permissive* will of God. The permissive will simply means that God is "permitting" you to function in the manner you are operating, even though it is not ultimately His divine plan for your life. When you are in His permissive will, it means that you ignored, disregarded, or selected the path that He presented to you during various times in your life and chose to take a different path. The path to God does not look pleasing at first, which is why it is the less traveled path. It looks hard and requires self-denial, self-sacrifice and self-discipline, but in the end, there is fullness of joy. It is in His *perfect* will that you find your purpose, your assignment and your place in Him.

TAILOR-MADE TESTS

In the world ye shall have tribulation: but be of good cheer, I have overcome the world (John 16:33). No one is exempt from being visited by tribulation and trouble. At some point in life, you will either be in a test, coming out of one, or getting ready to go into one. These unwanted visitors will come knocking on your door at the worst times and if you choose not to answer, they will knock the door down and come right on in; but they do not stay forever. They will at some point leave, and you are not the same person when they do. They leave a lesson to be learned from their visit. Jesus tried to prepare us for this in the scripture above. Tests, trials and temptations will come, but the way in which we respond to them determines our outcome. Tests and trials are designed to make us stronger, to examine our fortitude, and to make us wiser. A very large portion of our wisdom and strength comes from eating the bread of adversity and drinking the waters of affliction. We acquire knowledge and wisdom from the trials and tests, not the victories and triumphs. There is always a hidden lesson to be found in every test. Your most triumphant stories will come from your struggles. The seeds of your successes are in your failures. Your praises are birthed from your pain. Keep standing. I have never seen a storm last forever. It comes to pass. Seasons change. Be encouraged today.

God does test us. He has to test the faith that we claim we have in Him, but He does not tempt us. Presenting us with temptations is not part of God's character. Temptation is Satan's mode of operation for the people of God. *Let no man say when he is tempted, I am tempted of God: for God cannot be tempted with evil, neither tempts he any man: but every man is tempted, when he is drawn away of his own lust, and enticed (James 1:13-15).* When God desires to take us to the next spiritual level, we must pass our tailor-made test first. It is somewhat likened to school. In order to pass to the next grade, a cumulative test is given. If you pass the test, you are "promoted" to the next grade level. If you fail the test, you must "repeat" the same grade and take the same test all over again. No one is ever just taken to a higher level without passing the test. The cost in the natural could be: attentively listening to your teachers, diligently studying the coursework and making hard, but necessary sacrifices. The cost in the spirit could be attentively listening to the Word of God as it goes forth, diligently studying the sacred scriptures, making hard, but necessary sacrifices, praying constantly and fasting. In order to get to another level, you must conquer another devil. When you past the test in the natural, God will bless you in the spirit, but if you fail the test in the natural, you must do your first work all over again. Life is too short to be going around and around the same mountain of trial. Even though your cross is heavy, don't stop carrying it. Sometimes our tests and trials come as a result of what we ourselves have asked for. God does not answer prayers in the manner that we think He should or would. We ask and pray for things, but what we desire is already inside of us waiting to be awakened and called forth. We just don't get them in the manner we think they should come. For instance, when you ask for strength, you may get heartache and pain from which you grow stronger. When you ask for wisdom, you may get problems that require wise judgments in order to solve. When you ask for courage, you may get dangers to overcome. When you ask for riches, you may taste poverty for a season in order to appreciate your riches when they arrive. When you ask for God's anointing, you may go through a severe wilderness experience. You must pay a price for what you receive, but the power to acquire those things is already inside of you. There is a blessing for the pressing.

THE WILDERNESS

At some point in the Christian's life, a wilderness experience will come, and it seems to come at the most inopportune times - when things are going well in your career, finances, business, family-wise, relationships, etc. Your life becomes instantaneously interrupted, turned upside down and you are thrown into the wilderness. One day you are doing well and the next day you seem to be in hell. It feels as though you have been uprooted, snatched out, and all of your comforts are removed. Your life all of a sudden becomes chaotic, confused and out of sync. This is because when it's time to be elevated, God has to take you out of your comfort zone and away from what is familiar so you will have no choice but to depend on Him. This is a necessary process in earning the anointing. Needless-to-say, no one wants to go through the wilderness because it is a very lonely and humbling place to be. It is a place of isolation, a place where you are alienated and alone. People do not understand what is happening to you and in you, so there is no need in trying to explain how you feel. Only God understands. Some days you are up and other days you are extremely down. The wilderness is a place of extremes, no balance. You can never get comfortable in the wilderness. However, while you are uncomfortable, you are growing. The wilderness is a place of irritation and discomfort, and you cannot take anyone with you. You must go by yourself, but it is in the wilderness when God reveals Himself to you through your total dependence upon Him. He authenticates you, anoints you, and proves Himself to be your Father. He prepares you and teaches you things that you could not learn in the natural. While in the wilderness, self has to die. It is there where He tests your heart and your faithfulness. He gives you a new heart and a new mind in the wilderness. When you come out, you are a totally different person and people can see it all over you. The weight of His glory rests upon you and the anointing on your life is powerful and penetrating because you have paid the price for it. You need misery in order to have a legitimate ministry. Out of your misery, your ministry is birthed. Your growth is determined by your ability to keep walking through the valley of the *shadow* of death. It is just a shadow! It is not death. It is not real. It is not the final analysis of your life. It is only a shadow! It has been said that Satan builds a man up so that He can tear him down, but God has to tear a man down first so He can build him up. In God, you are always victorious!

Between the promise and the Promised Land is a wilderness experience which is the exact opposite of what you have been promised. Israel was promised a land flowing with milk and honey, but in their initial wanderings, there was not even water. When they did finally enter the Promised Land, they were given homes that they did not build, cisterns that they did not dig and vineyards that they did not plant. God will do the same for you, but you must first go through the wilderness. How long you spend there is up to you. You can praise your way out of it, or prolong your time there through murmuring and complaining. An eight-day journey turned into 40 years for the Israelites. Take heed.

As I write this book, I find myself in the wilderness. My entire life has been shaken from its foundation. At the moment, I do not know what to do or where to turn. All I know to do is pray, praise, worship, and study the Word of God for guidance. I am confident that God is refining me, purging and purifying me for something that my natural eyes cannot see. In this fire, it is hot, burns, and is painful. I am up at times and down at other times, but my faith in God is unshaken because I know that He will never leave me nor forsake me. He never has. It is needful that I endure this "light affliction". His Word is true and cannot and will not return back to Him void. I therefore hold on to the promises that He has spoken over my life. I know that in this life, we are sure to have trials and tribulations, victories and triumphs, up and downs. But each situation is designed to make you stronger, build you up and turn you towards God. God tests His people, tries our faith, proves us and sees whether we will shrink in the time of trial. He already knows how we will test, but He needs us to be able to see and know ourselves. We think we know ourselves, but God has to sometimes show us who we really are. YOU must be able to see yourself for who you really are! Your tests are not designed to kill you, but to reveal you. The rewards of this life come to those who overcome and do not crumble in the face of adversity. They persevere and press forward in spite of what they face. Your problems do have an expiration date! You are more than a conqueror. I rejoice in where I'm going because I know that I will not be in this wilderness forever. This too shall pass and by faith, I am entering into a season of new beginnings. By faith, I am triumphantly victorious because I am a child of the King. What father will stand by and permit His child to continue to suffer forever? Not our Heavenly Father. He is a Healer and a Deliverer and He will never leave us alone. God has given us sufficient evidence of His love and we are not to doubt His goodness because we do not understand the workings of His providence. He will make all things new again.

THIS "LIGHT" AFFLICTION

Everyone will endure hardships and disappointments at some point in life, but in the Word of God, these are referred to as "light afflictions." To us, it seems very hard and we wonder how much longer we must suffer, but God who, in His infinite wisdom looks at everything from the perspective of eternity says, "This is a light affliction and you have only endured for a moment." *For our light affliction, which is but for a moment, works for us a far more exceeding and eternal weight of glory; while we look not at the things which are seen, but at the things which are not seen: for the things which are seen are temporal; but the things which are not seen are eternal (2 Corinthians 4:17-19).* God says that your affliction is "light" and after it passes away, it leaves space for blessings to fill the space. When you come out on the other side, the afflictions you suffered seems to be but a faded memory, but you are not to forget how you felt as you were in the fire. It is necessary that you keep in mind how you felt and what you felt, so that you can minister to others as they go through similar tests and trials that you have already experienced. Always remember that there is always something good that comes out of every adversity and pain. We must not let the pain blind us from recognizing the good. Every successful person has a painful story. Every painful story has a successful ending, so accept the pain and get ready for the success!

Your experiences are not just designed for you, but for you to be a valuable contributor to the body of Christ through your testimonies. God designs life so that, in His divine providence, when you testify of your story and how He brought you out, you will bless and encourage someone listening. The righteous are placed in the furnace of fire so that they may be purified. The fire is hot. It burns and is painful, but it is necessary for purification. Being in the "fire of affliction" is likened unto gold. The longer that gold is placed in the heat, the brighter it shines. The more you put fire to gold, the purer it becomes. Each time it goes into the fire, more impurities are removed. You will be placed in the furnace of fire, but you will not burn up, you will not smell like smoke when you come out and the light of God's glory will shine in you as a light that is set upon a hill. There are two things that will motivate you in life: pain and pleasure. We must use pain for the purpose it was created: to move you forward in life. Everyone has a different threshold for pain. Pain was never designed to kill you, but rather to reveal you. How you respond to pain shows what you are made of. The Lord's eye is upon His people and His ear is open to their cries. Your affliction seems great and the flames of the furnace seem as though they are going to consume you, but the Refiner will bring you forth as gold tried in the fire. Sometimes God calms the storm and sometimes He calms His child to be able to go through the storm. God's love for His children during the period of our severest trial is as strong and tender as in the days of our sunniest prosperity, but it is necessary for us to be placed in the furnace of fire because our earthliness must be consumed so that the image of Christ may be perfectly reflected in us. Your destiny is bigger than your current circumstance!

THE LIGHT OF KNOWLEDGE

You awaken to a new reality when you discover the will of God for your life. Satan does not want you to walk in the light of knowledge because when you do, you become empowered. It is his desire that we all be ignorant of God's will and plan for our individual lives. Ignorance is a disease, but knowledge is the cure. As long as you do not know *who* you are and *whose* you are, you are walking in darkness and Satan doesn't bother you as much, but when you enter the light of the knowledge of Jesus Christ and the veil is lifted from your eyes as to God's will for your life, you become empowered and impregnated. All hell and high water seems to break loose in your life at the very moment you step into the light of that knowledge. You enter spiritual battles that are set up to kill your spirit, steal your joy, and destroy your hope in Christ. A designated set of demons are sent on assignment to assault you. When this happens, you are officially in spiritual warfare, but the good news is that you will prevail! You are more than a conqueror in Him who loves you (Romans 8:37).

It is the objective of Satan to cause a spiritual miscarriage so that you will not bring forth that "holy thing" that God has placed inside you. That "holy thing" is your ministry. Satan wants to kill that baby; but rest assured that you have angels fighting battles for you in the spirit realm. You are not alone, but you too must enter warfare. Your prayers, your fasting, your study of the scriptures are all spiritual weapons that you use to help you fight. Your weapons are not carnal, they are spiritual. It is the objective of Satan to kill the seed that you are impregnated with. His ultimate goal is to murder, cause a spiritual miscarriage, intercept the manifestation or cause you to abort what God has placed inside you. When you enter spiritual warfare, you cannot rely on the warring archangels to fight everything for you without you fighting for yourself. If they do all of your fighting alone, the manifestation could take longer than expected. Your faith decides diving timing. You at some point must enter battle. Gird up your lions! Put on the whole armor our God (Ephesians 6) and go into spiritual warfare with warfare prayers, fasting, interceding, supplicating, and studying the scriptures. God will let you see the enemy and his tactics.

In order to conquer your enemy, you must know its name, mode of operation and find the unguarded gates in your own fortress where he is gaining entrance. You are not fighting with flesh and blood. You are fighting with invisible forces. *For we wrestle not against flesh and blood, but against principalities, against powers, against the rulers of the darkness of this world, against spiritual wickedness in high places (Ephesians 6:12).* Crying, complaining, talking about it or worrying about it is not going to conquer it. God does not move in our emotions. He moves by our acts of faith. You cannot fight the spiritual with the natural! That which is flesh is flesh, and that which is spirit is spirit. The battle is not as long as it appears to be in the natural realm, but the cost being paid while fighting this spiritual fight is what brings forth the anointing of God in you. It is through the fire, enduring the tribulations, and staying on your knees that brings forth that sweet-smelling aroma to God. I do not know how hot it has been in your life lately, but I smell a fresh anointing coming out of you!

CHAPTER ENDING WISDOM KEYS

◆ When the narrow path is chosen, it leads to peace, joy, prosperity, and eternal life; but the narrow path requires self-discipline. The Christian's life should be a disciplined life.

◆ No two paths are the same for any two people. You cannot go where God has predestinated someone else to go no matter how bad you may want to.

◆ We sometimes veer off onto an unmarked path that leads to a dead end. It is at this time that we must detour our way back to the starting place and choose another path.

◆ Your relationship with God must be real and true, alive and active, constant and consistent. That relationship must consist of prayer, praise, worship and study of the sacred scriptures.

◆ I do not know how hot it has been in your life lately, but I smell a fresh anointing coming out of you!

Chapter 2
The Fullness of Time

But when the fullness of time was come, God sent forth His Son, made of a woman, made under the law, to redeem them that were under the law, that we might receive the adoption of sons.

(Galatians 4:4-5)

Walking in the knowledge of God's will for your life gives you a sense of confidence in Him and increases your faith and assurance that He has a carefully mapped out plan for your life. However, many make the mistake of thinking that once they get the revelation of God's plan for their life, the next day, they should get the manifestation. For this reason, the Lord encourages us in Philippians 4:6-7 to, *be anxious for nothing; but in everything by prayer and supplication with thanksgiving let your requests be made known unto God. And the peace of God, which passes all understanding, shall keep your hearts and minds through Christ Jesus.* Because we live in a microwave, on-demand society, we want everything instantly, but God cannot and will not be rushed. He is a Master Planner and operates according to seasons and times. It may not be your season for manifestation just yet, so trying to make things happen right away can cause severe consequences. Although you may know what you have been called to do, it is crucial that you wait until the right season to do it. Once God's revelation about you has taken root in your heart, then the foundation has been laid broad and deep, firm and true; but a preparation time is needful and mandatory. The time between the revelation and the manifestation is an essential time for preparing yourself for the place the Lord is taking you. Too many have stepped out before the perfect time and have become cheap imitations of others. They were not ready. They were half-baked and taken out of the oven too soon, then presented to the people to partake of. The people then spit out what is served to them, because it is bitter. Stepping out before God's timing has caused many to fall a hard and humiliating fall. For this reason, the Lord admonishes us to be patient and wait. *But they that wait upon the Lord shall renew their strength; they shall mount up with wings as eagles; they shall run, and not be weary; and they shall walk, and not faint (Isaiah 40:31).*

THE ANOINTING AND THE APPOINTING

David was about 20 years old when Samuel anointed him as king, but it wasn't until he was 30 years old that he took the throne. There was a ten-year wait before the fullness of time had come. Saul was king during the time that David was anointed to be the next king. After the anointing, David could have tried to take the throne from Saul by his own hand, but being a wise young man, he did not. Even though God had rejected Saul at this point, David knew not to rise up against anything or anyone that God had anointed. He allowed the Lord, in His divine timing and providence to let the unfolding of events happen, which placed David in the king's palace at the right time. The time between David's *anointing* and his *appointing*, or his revelation and manifestation, was an extremely difficult time for him. He had to dwell in caves running from Saul in order to preserve his life.

It is the same way with us. The time between the anointing and the appointing can be a very harsh wilderness experience. King Saul tried to kill David in order to keep him from becoming king, just as King Herod tried to kill Jesus to keep Him from becoming king. Satan, using Saul, desired to have David killed in order to cause a spiritual murder, miscarriage, or abortion of the "holy thing" that God had placed inside David. In this case, David's "holy thing" was to be the next King, ruler and warrior of Israel. David stayed on his face before the Lord and was led of the Lord's Spirit until the fullness of time had come. Before taking the throne, God protected David, lead him, and guided him through all dangers, toils and discouragements that he was enduring by the hand of Saul. There is no glory without a story. If you want the anointing, then accept the appointing. Within the time between David's anointing and his appointing, he was being prepared to become king. He may not have known it at the time, but God strategically placed him in a position where he could see and learn how to run a kingdom. He had lived in the king's palace, saw how the king conducted business, became knowledgeable of the intricacies and logistics of operating a kingdom and learned protocol of kingdom business. He was getting prepared for the next level. It is no different with us as children of God. As a child of God, the enemy desires to kill what is inside of you as well. You are no different from anyone else who has brought forth a powerful ministry. Every great person has a story to tell. There is no glory without a story and no test without a testimony. Maximizing the time between the calling and the commission is essential.

A LESSON ON GROWING IMPATIENT

We do not need to "help" God in carrying out His will for our lives. He does not need nor want our help. Disastrous things can happen when we grow impatient in waiting on the Lord. Abraham is a perfect example of this. He had been given the revelation from the angel of God that he would bring forth a son out of his own loins, and through him shall all the nations of the earth be blessed, but after waiting so long and looking at things in the natural (his age and Sarah's age), he began to rely upon his own human reasoning and decided to "help" God. As a result of this, Ishmael was born, which was of the flesh. Subsequently, Isaac was born, who was of the Spirit. Just as there has been enmity between the Arabs, which are Ishmael's descendants and the Jews, Isaac's descendants, there will always be enmity between that which is born of the flesh and that which is born of the Spirit. Abraham's impatience has been a historical devastating reality that is wreaking international havoc in the world even today. Our impatience or desire to "help" God can cause us a great deal of misery. It is better to wait on God. Those who wait on His perfect timing before stepping out, become great and powerful men and women.

    Single Christians often have made this same mistake. They grow impatient in waiting for the Lord to send them a mate, so they resort to compromise. Against their intuition and the promptings of the Holy Spirit, they attach themselves to a person who ends up causing them a world of grief, anguish and hurt. They choose a mate out of their human desires and reasoning, and then present the person before the Lord to bless the union. We cannot rely on our human reasoning to "help" God by bringing him an unsanctified offering and asking Him to bless it. God does not bless mess! We must ask for more patience if that is what is needed, but we must not grow impatient and start making life-changing decisions on our own. All believers have done it, but through mistakes, we learn and grow. *Wait on the LORD: be of good courage, and he shall strengthen thine heart: wait, I say, on the LORD (Psalm 27:14).*

SEASONS

Be not weary in well-doing, for in DUE SEASON, you shall reap, "if" you faint not (Galatians 6:9). Just as the earth goes through various seasons, so does your life. Learn to discern. When the time comes to step out on faith, you must not delay. Delayed obedience is disobedience. Do not let the timing pass you by and cause you to miss your divine appointment. Know the seasons and when your time comes, leap out on faith. In order to know your season, observe what is happening in you and around you. God will catch you when you leap out in faith if the timing is in His will. Life is about growth and change. You are always in a season. The season could be planting time, reaping time, or waiting time. Be mindful of the present moment and know the current season. In the sowing season, you are busy working and preparing for what's next. During this season, you are tired and overwhelmed at times. Be sure that in the midst of your busyness, you are sowing good seeds so that when harvest comes, you will receive a bountiful harvest from what you have sown. The reaping season is the season of your harvest. This could be a time when showers of blessings are raining down upon you like the dew falling to refresh the earth. Things are going well and it appears that everything you touch is being blessed. Phone calls with good news are flooding in. Mailbox blessings are manifesting, promotions are being offered and you are being elevated. The good seeds that you have sown have fully matured, multiplied and are now materializing in your life. You can only have a harvest of good things if you have sown good seeds. For some, right now may be a season of harvest; for others, a season of reaping the negative and corrupted seeds they have sown. For others, it could be the season to watch, pray, and stand still. Stay vigilant. Just as the shift in the atmosphere represents a change in seasons, you too are shifting, which represents a change in your life. Allow yourself to transition naturally into your new season, whatever it may be right now. Old things are passing away. All things are becoming new.

There is also a season for letting things go. If you hold on to things when it is time to let them go, you may not have room for the new and the better when you enter your new season. Let things, people, issues, pain, unforgiveness, situations, and problems go when it is time for them to leave. You cannot hold on to something forever. If you try to make things stay when it is time to let them go, then your weakness gets stronger. Your strength gets weaker. Know when the time has come to release. In order to get the new, you must release the old. Even Satan works in seasons. After Jesus' 40 day fast, the devil tempted Him three times. As Jesus resisted every temptation, the Word of God says, *...and when the devil had ended all the temptations, he departed from him for a **season** (Luke 4:13)*. God has you where you are right now for a reason and for a season. Let things run their course. When the fullness of time comes, it all works together for your good!

TEMPTATIONS

The Bible is filled with wisdom, biblical symbolisms, lessons to be learned, prophecies and practices, and if studied with an open heart for the truth, rays of light will shine to the understanding. The life of Jesus on earth is an example that it is possible to live a life of obedience. In His earthly life, Jesus had unwavering integrity, a humble spirit, gentle manners, and earnest and sincere piety. He exemplified in His life the precepts which He taught. As we study the Word of God, we apply spiritual principles to our lives and allow the lessons to take root in us. In the book of Luke, chapter 4, we clearly see the tactic that Satan uses to tempt the people of God. He comes in a methodical, well-planned out manner to manipulate and deceive the children of

God; and if we are not careful, we can fall right into his snare. In this chapter, we see that Satan tries to tempt our Savior three times, in three different ways, using three different offers. The temptations were in the following three areas:

1. **Identity**
   Bait: Using basic needs

2. **Worship**
   Bait: Using worldly pleasures

3. **The calling**
   Bait: Using the Word of God

When we analyze the chapter, we see clearly the three areas of temptation. Jesus had just come off of a 40-day fast and was hungry. It was during this time that Satan came to tempt Him in the very area where He was weak, which was His basic need for food. He challenged Jesus' identity to strengthen the temptation. His plan was to compel Jesus to prove Himself. *"If you are the son of God, command this stone that it may be made bread" (Luke 4:3).* He comes at us in the same manner, challenging our identity in Christ when we are weak in the area of basic needs. Those basic needs could be money, food, shelter, security, clothes, affection or companionship. Wherever you may be weak or vulnerable, Satan will come and try to make you an offer in that specific area. His scheme is to approach the children of God at their most vulnerable time and make them question their identity in Christ. *If God loved you so much, then why is He allowing you to suffer like this?; If you were really His child, He would not have allowed you to lose your job; If God cared about you, then why are you broke and have no money for bills?* etc. His tactic has not changed from the day he tempted Jesus in the wilderness; and our response to him should not change either. How did Jesus respond to Satan? With the Word of God! His response to Satan in this area was, *It is written that man shall not live by bread alone, but by every Word of God" (Luke 4:4).*

The second temptation was to offer Jesus worldly pleasures and material things in exchange for His worship to Satan. *"All this power will I give thee and the glory of them ...if thou therefore will worship me" (Luke 4:7).* Satan causes us to look at our earthly condition in order to make us feel that we are in lack. He then attempts to allure us with the immediate gratifications of our flesh. Many of God's children fall for it. They love houses, money and possessions more than they love God. The invitation to worship Satan is seldom blatant enough to be perceived as such. It is usually an invitation to take the wider more traveled road. Again, how did Jesus respond to Satan? With the Word of God! His response to Satan in this area was, *It is written that thou shall worship the Lord thy God and Him only shall thou serve (Luke 4:8).* Jesus did not entertain the offer, but rather came back with the Word only.

Satan desires your worship as well. When he was a covering cherub in heaven, he was in the throne room and witnessed the Father and the Son receiving praise and worship from the heavenly beings. He desired that same praise and worship for himself. Lucifer said, *I will exalt my throne above the stars of God; ...I will be like the most High (Isaiah 14:13).* This is what caused his great fall from grace. He was not satisfied being third in line. He wanted to take part in the counsels of God with His son concerning the plans for mankind. He sought to gain control of the heavenly angels, to draw them away from their Creator, and to win their reverence to himself. Of course God did not permit this rebellion in heaven and cast Satan, along with the rebelling angels out of heaven. *I beheld Satan as lightning fall from heaven (Luke 10:18).* He continues to use deception and lies to bring worship to him because he knows that humans were created to worship. Without any intellectual or theological awareness, man instinctively was created to worship, and if we do not purposely and willingly choose to Worship the God of heaven and earth, the King of Kings and Lord of Lords, then we will worship something or someone else. Satan wants to divert the minds of the people of God from their Creator so that we will worship the creature instead of the Creator. As long as you are not worshipping God, Satan is fine, because that makes it easier to end up worshipping him. That is the second area of temptation, to steal your worship from God.

    The third manner in which he tempted Jesus was to try and get him to abort his calling by using the Word of God. Using scripture to support his stance, he tried to get Jesus to throw Himself off of a high mountain. Had Jesus jumped, man would have been doomed for eternity. There would have been no Golgotha experience, no Holy Spirit sent to comfort us, and no love of God shed abroad in our hearts. We would have been eternally separated from God. How did Jesus respond to this last temptation? With the Word of God! His response to Satan in this area was, *It is written that thou shall not tempt the Lord thy God (Luke 4:12).* This is no different than what he does with us. He creeps up and whispers in the ear telling some to commit suicide, to step out into a position before the time, to go left when God is guiding them to go right; to pry a door open that has been locked, when God has an open door for them to walk through. Satan wants the people of God distracted from higher purposes and away from the will of God for our lives. He wants us in the wrong place at the wrong time doing the wrong thing. His strategy has not changed, but if we resist his temptations and use the Word of God as our weapon as Jesus did, he will eventually leave - for a season. *And when the devil had ended all the temptations, he* *departed from him for a **season**.* Then the angels of God will come to minister to us.

A MESSAGE FOR ASPIRING SPIRITUAL LEADERS

In order to walk in true spiritual authority, God Himself has to train you. You must have an encounter with Him before you can proclaim the Gospel of Jesus Christ. You do not become a leader first and get trained later. You do not preach first and encounter God later. Things must be done decently and in order. God is a God of order. There are no shortcuts to anointed ministry. You must go through God first. It is He who authenticates you and fills you with His Spirit. Titles and degrees may command the respect of the world, but they do not impress God. He cares nothing about your degrees, but He does care about your degree in Him. Many professions of religion in the present day are lovers of the world, conformers to the world, lovers of comfort and aspirers after respectability. They can be found in almost every church. For this reason, the heavenly Teacher has often passed by the great men of the earth, the prominent, the titled, the degreed, and the wealthy who are used to receiving respect and praise and rests His spirit upon the humble, pious and teachable. Our intellectual powers should be held as a gift from our Maker and should be used in the service of truth and righteousness; but when pride and ambition are cherished, and men exalt their own theories above the Word of God, then intelligence can accomplish greater harm than ignorance. This is why God chooses the humble, meek and teachable. Only He Himself, through His Spirit can teach you spiritual things. Formal teaching is fine, in fact it is admirable, but it is God Himself who reveals the treasures of truth to your understanding. You do not learn those treasures in even the finest Bible Colleges. You must take and pass The Master's course.

The Fullness of Time

After you have endured the tests, overcome the trials, been through the fire, and resisted the temptations, the fullness of time will come. God will reveal to you that the season has arrived for you to step out and begin your ministry. You have been patient in waiting, diligent in study and wise in preparing; now the time has come for you to bring forth your ministry. Those who have been trained by the Lord, will bring forth good fruit that will be sweet, pleasant and refreshing to the soul. They have earned their B.A. Degree from God. They are now **B**orn **A**gain! We will know you by your fruit. *A good tree cannot bring forth corrupt fruit, neither can a corrupt three bring forth good fruit (Mathew 7:18).* As a true servant of the Lord, you will stand out as a lamp set upon a hill. You will not be able to hide the light and glory of God that shines within you. You will be set apart from those who cling to customs and traditions and you will be drawn to those who stand by a living relationship with the Lord.

BY THEIR FRUIT YOU SHALL KNOW THEM

Many modern churches of the day have been decimated by a lack of discipline and self-control, but a problem perhaps more destructive is the uncanny knack for accepting weak, Christian leaders. More often than not, this is done because these leaders appear to be preeminent in dignity and strength. Their impressive credentials make them attractive and their charismatic personality seals the deal. A high salary is paid for a talented preacher to entertain and attract the people. Their sermons do not touch popular sins, but are smooth and pleasing for fashionable ears. Thus, fashionable sinners are enrolled on the church records, and fashionable sins are concealed under a pretense of Godliness. It suits the policy of Satan that men should retain the "forms" of religion if but the Spirit of vital Godliness is missing. This is not to advocate choosing those who are physically weak or intellectually challenged, but the point is not to judge solely on externals, but be led of the Spirit of God as to whom He has chosen for the present time. We must understand that natural strength, impressive degrees or social connections are not requirements for spiritual leadership. Too often, religious leaders who are thus praised and reverenced lose sight of their dependence upon God and are led to trust in themselves. Titles, degrees and a charismatic personality cannot bring forth the gifts of the spirit.

    Your ministry is your function, not your rank. The call to authority is the call to serve. In heaven, rank is earned by humility, service and love. The deacon who loves more is higher than the apostle who loves less. God has made ministers the depositaries of His holy Word. What have we done with the light and truth given us to make believers wise unto salvation? No value is attached to a mere "profession" of faith in Christ; only the love which is shown by works is counted genuine. Yet it is love alone which in the sight of heaven makes any act of value. Whatever is done from love, however small it may appear in the estimation of men, is accepted and rewarded of God. Spiritual leaders are called to feed the flock of God, not to set up their own flocks. They are not called to teach about Jesus, but to allow Jesus to teach through them. Some get confused and caught up in their titles that they veer away from Jesus and eventually lose their way. Their focus becomes distorted and the objective of saving souls from the grips of sin and flames of hell is lost. The great commission is the winning of souls to Christ by teaching the message of faith in God and salvation through Christ Jesus. Every ministry should be centered solely and earnestly around that. However, traditions and customs of men have taken the place of winning lost souls to God. Instead of steadfastly imparting a true and living Word to the sheep, churches have focused their attention on programs, church anniversaries, pastors' appreciations, pastors' birthdays, first-fruit conferences, building fund drives, women's/men's conferences, revivals and banquets. The foundational purpose of preaching and teaching on God's redemptive plan to save humanity has gotten lost and buried somewhere between the programs and the revivals. The gospel of Christ cannot be preached without offense, but since there has been a widespread conformity to the world's standards, the church awakens no opposition. Traditions and customs have become exalted. There is a danger in exalting human theories above the Word of God. Ceremonies of the church and good works are powerless to atone for sin. The religion that is current today is not of the pure and holy character that marked the Christian faith in the days of Christ and His apostles. It is because of the spirit of compromise with the world that has been embraced. A "profession" of religion has become popular with the world. Politicians, rulers, lawyers, doctors and public servants join the church as a means of securing the respect and confidence of society while advancing their own worldly interests. Thus, many of them seek to cover all of their unrighteous transactions under a "profession" of Christianity. When Satan cannot fully get his way with the people of God, he resorts to compromise which leads to apostasy.

PROTECT YOUR ANOINTING

The price that you will have paid to walk in the anointing is too high to risk losing. Once your ministry is birthed, you will be functioning in a higher spiritual realm, but the stakes get higher and the temptations become more appealing. In order to stay focused and strong, you must stay on your knees in prayer and absorb yourself in the Word of God constantly, otherwise, the devil, in his subtleness will sift you as wheat. You must seek the

Lord daily because as you stand before the sheep of God, you must be able to feed them an on-time, in season Word, fresh from Heaven. Wherever the unadulterated and uncompromised gospel is received, the minds of the people are awakened. They begin to cast off the shackles that had them bondslaves of ignorance, sin, and superstition and they begin to think and act as men and women of God. The only way you can do that is by staying in His presence and allowing Him to drop His message for His people into your spirit. Otherwise, you will begin to feel that you no longer need to study the Word of God in order to stand before His people. The enemy will have you thinking that you are so anointed that you can take an old sermon, dress it up and feed it to the people, or that you can take a scripture, add a few points to it, then hoop and shout in order to entertain the flesh of the people. If you get to a point where you are no longer seeking the Lord for guidance as to what to say to His sheep from the pulpit, then your teaching/preaching will become stale. You will be nothing more than a sounding brass and tinkling symbol. Beyond jumping and shouting, the people of God need a solid, life-changing Word to help the hurting in their souls. A hoop and a shout cannot heal them, but the unadulterated, uncompromised, unwatered down Word of God can. If you have been called to preach or teach, then be a faithful teacher of the truth. One cannot speak a pure Word from the Lord until they are delivered from the fear of man and the desire for man's recognition and acceptance. The person who fears God rather than man will always be perceived as a threat to man and his interests.

RECOGNIZE THE LORD'S VOICE

There are no shortcuts to anointed ministry! As an anointed spiritual leader, you must be able to recognize the Lord's voice when He speaks. He does not always speak in the same manner. He comes in different forms so that you will be able to recognize Him by the Spirit regardless of what manner He comes in. This is why you must know Him by the Spirit. He is a lion and He is also a lamb. The Scriptures say that He came to bring peace, but He also came to bring a sword. These different aspects of the Lord's nature do not contradict each other, rather they complement each other and give us a more complete revelation of His character. When He comes as a lion, He may roar from Zion. When He comes as a lamb, He may whisper in a small still voice. If you are only use to hearing Him as a whisper, then you will miss Him when He roars from Zion and vice versa. After Jesus' ascension, He came to the disciples in different forms for 40 days. At first they did not recognize Him. He did this so that they would get use to knowing Him by His spirit and not by any outward form. He does the same with us. If we only judge by outward appearances, we will miss Him when He comes in the form of a vagabond, bag lady, street sweeper or prisoner, but if we know the Lord by the Spirit, we will recognize Him regardless of the manner or form in which He comes. Every believer should know the Lord's voice.

CHAPTER ENDING WISDOM KEYS

- We do not need to "help" God in carrying out His will for our lives. He does not need nor want our help. Disastrous things can happen when we grow impatient in waiting on the Lord.

- Delayed obedience is disobedience. Do not let the timing pass you by and cause you to miss your divine appointment. Know the seasons and when your time comes, leap out on faith.

- Spiritual leaders are called to feed the flock of God, not to set up their own flocks. They are not called to teach about Jesus, but to allow Jesus to teach through them.

- You must seek the Lord daily because as you stand before the sheep of God, you must be able to feed them an on-time, in season Word fresh from Heaven. The only way you can do that is by staying in His presence and allowing Him to drop His message into your spirit.

- Fashionable sinners are enrolled on the church records, and fashionable sins are concealed under a pretense of Godliness. It suits the policy of Satan that men should retain the "forms" of religion if but the Spirit of vital Godliness is missing.

Chapter 3
Stepping Into Destiny

> ...moreover whom he did predestinate, them He also called: and whom he called, them he also justified: and whom he justified, them he also glorified.
>
> *(Romans 8:30)*

As we grow in wisdom, knowledge and spiritual understanding, we begin to realize that the things we once thought were so important to us, really do not matter anymore. As our relationship with God grows deeper, we begin to see more clearly with the eyes of the heart than we do with the natural eyes. Saul had to become blind in the natural so that he could see in the Spirit. At some point in life, we must become blind in the natural in order to clearly see in the spirit as well. Lift up your eyes. Go beyond the natural and see what's in the Spirit. Faith is increased with spiritual vision. This is why Abraham was able to believe God - because he had spiritual insight. He saw things in the Spirit that the natural person could not see. His faith was strong because he trusted in the things that were not seen more than the things that were seen. Once the spiritual vision becomes clear, the heart's desire is heavenly bound instead of earthly bound. Spiritual vision develops wisdom in the seeker. The Word of God tells us in Proverbs 4:7 that, *wisdom is the principle thing, therefore get wisdom, and in all thy getting, get understanding.*

Many desire wisdom, and some even think they have it, but the wisdom they have is not of the pure, Godly wisdom that sets men free and brings peace. Ideally, wisdom "should" come with age, but it sometimes does not. Common sense is not the same as wisdom either. Some people have street sense with no wisdom. Intellect does not mean the same thing as wisdom. There are many educated fools. Change does not bring about wisdom and neither does time. There are 80 year-old fools and 15 year-old wise Christians. The study of the scriptures with an earnest and prayerful heart combined with a living relationship with the Lord produces Godly wisdom. The application of biblical principles produces prosperity. There are three different kinds of wisdom: human wisdom, worldly wisdom, and Godly wisdom. We must be sure that the wisdom we *think* we have is tested by the weight of the sacred scriptures. *But the wisdom that is from above is first pure, then peaceable, gentle, and easy to be intreated, full of mercy and good fruits, without partiality, and without hypocrisy (James 3:17).* Godly wisdom comes with an appreciation for the tests and trials that were overcome; a giving of thanks for the purification process resulting from being in the furnace of fire, a heart of praise for the strengthened character emerged from betrayals, and a humble heart produced from rejection. Wisdom teaches the valuable lessons learned through each experience and allows those lessons to make us stronger and wiser.

  Entering wisdom leads the children of God to look back over their lives and remember, rededicate, rejoice, and renew. As the hard tests and trials that were overcome are contemplated, wisdom reveals that every believer must be tested on what they profess to believe. You must be the first partaker of what you teach, preach or believe. Both the tests and the devil's temptations will come in one or all of those three areas. Tests do not come in areas that have no affect on you. They come in the areas you profess to have the most faith in. Temptation is not a lasting condition. It is a passing phase, and once it is conquered, it ceases to be a temptation. Satan is not going to tempt you on your shout or your song, he will tempt you on your belief in the Word. You claim that you are standing on the Word of God? Satan says, *Let me turn up the heat in her life and let's see just how long she will hold on to God's Word!* You say you have faith in God? Satan says, *Let's see how much faith she really has after her home goes into foreclosure, her car is repossessed and her husband tells her he wants a divorce.* You will be tempted on what you profess to believe. Wisdom reveals that.

REMEMBER

God will never leave, forsake, nor forget about His children. As you look back over your life, can't you see that God never left you even though there were times when you thought He had? He proved Himself to be right there all along. Every trial and tribulation that you thought was the end of your world passed away, and you were alright when it was all over. Those situations that you thought you would never come out of, are but a faded memory today, but you are still here, still standing and still holding on to God's unchanging Hand. God is faithful. He hears the prayers of the heart and He wipes away tears. We must never forget what God has done for us because it gives us the assurance in knowing that He will always be there. He will not share His glory with another. This is why He sometimes delivers you at the 11th hour. That way, there will be no doubt that the supernatural intervention that manifested on your behalf came from God and God alone. No flesh shall glory in His sight. We do not remember our past afflictions in order to keep us down, but to keep us faithful and humble. Our remembrance should serve as a reminder of God's love and faithfulness to His children. Remembering how God brought you through the wilderness serves as a reminder that you are no longer there. Your latter days are so much better than your former. Let us never forget how far God has brought us.

REJOICE

When God sent Moses to Pharaoh to deliver the Israelites from under their cruel taskmaster, Moses asked the Lord what he should say when the Israelites ask him the name of the God who sent him to deliver them. And God said, *Thus shall you say unto the children of Israel, I AM has sent me to you (Exodus 3:13).* This is the first time that God had given Himself an identified name. Before this, He was simply referred to as 'The Lord' but He definitively identified Himself as "I AM" this time. Simply put, God is EVERYTHING we need Him to be to us, for us, and in us. You fill in the blanks. I am ___. I am___. I am ___. Here are a few fill-ins to help you: prosperous, healthy, wealthy, whole, healed, happy, encouraged, inspired, love, content, peaceful, etc. This is why in parts of the Bible, you will find these various statements: *Let the weak say, **I AM** strong (Joel 3:10); Let the poor say, **I AM** rich (Romans 4:17); Let the sick say, I AM healed (Isaiah 33:24).* Why should one speak contrary to their human condition? Because death and life are in the power of the tongue. You therefore do not have to confess your weakness in your humanity, but rather declare your strength, which is in divinity. We rejoice because that same "I AM" God is the same yesterday, today and forever. He changes not. We have access to Him and for this reason, we rejoice!

Although Exodus 3:13 was the first time that God gave Himself a designated name, the Bible is filled with various names for Him. Because God is infinite, we can never begin to describe everything that He is. We do know however, that everything He is, is good. Below are Hebrew translations for names of God described in the Old Testament. In prayer, we can call Him by some of these names according to what we need Him to be for us:

HEBREW NAMES FOR GOD

Adonai - Lord, Master (Gen 15:2)
El Elyon - The Most High God (Gen 14:18)
El Olam - The Everlasting God (Gen 21:33)
El Shaddai - The Lord God Almighty (Gen 17:1)
Elohim - The plural form of God (Gen 1:1)
Jehovah Jireh - The Lord who provides (Gen 22:14)
Jehovah Nissi - The Lord my banner (Exodus 17:15)
Jehovah Raah - The Lord My Shepherd (Psalm 23)
Jehovah Rapha - The Lord that heals (Exodus 15:26)
Jehovah Sabaoth - The Lord of Hosts (1Sa 1:3)
Jehovah Shalom - The Lord our peace (Judges 6:24)
Jehovah Shammah - The Lord is there (Ezekiel 48:35)
Jehovah Tsidkenu - The Lord our righteousness (Jer 23:6)

As we reflect on the fact that we have a crucified Redeemer who has paved the way for us to have access directly into the Father's presence, we rejoice. Christ was treated as we deserve so that we could be treated as He deserves. He was condemned for our sins, in which He had no share, so that we could be justified by His righteousness, in which we had no share. He suffered the death which was ours, so that we could receive the life which was His. What great love that is! We rejoice in knowing that Christ's sacrifice has appeased God's wrath that would have been reserved for us; His blood has washed away our impurities; His cross has taken on our curse; and His blood has atoned for us. Christ Jesus is our priest; His alter is our confessional and His blood is our sacrifice. We rejoice in knowing that we have a high priest who is always making intercession for us according to the will of God. *For we have not a high priest who cannot be touched with the feeling of our infirmities; but was in all points tempted like as we are, yet without sin. Let us therefore come boldly unto the throne of grace, that we may obtain mercy, and find grace to help in time of need (Hebrews 4:15-16).* We rejoice in knowing that He who is holy, harmless, undefiled, and separate from sinners is not ashamed to call us friends. Let us rejoice in the Lord always and again I say REJOICE!

REDEDICATE

In the book of Revelations (2:4), Christ tells us that we have left our first love. He is our first love, and at some point during our Christian walk, we let the fire on the candle of our love for Him grow dim. But when we repented, confessed our sins before the Father, renounced what caused us to turn away, and returned back into the Redeemer's loving arms with thankful hearts, we were cleansed from all unrighteousness. He stands with out-stretched arms inviting all to return to Him with their burdens of sins, cares and weariness. We are not saved in groups. Each must have their own intimate and personal relationship with the Lord. Each must confess their own sins and impurities from their own mouth. Let us rededicate ourselves to our first love!

Rededication develops in the heart and causes a return back to our first love, Jesus. The sacrifices of God are a broken spirit and a broken and contrite heart (Psalm 51:17). The life of the Christian should be a heart-searching, self-denying, self-emptying one. For this reason, we ask God to create in us a clean heart and renew a right spirit within us. Those who desire to be in right-standing before God, ask Him to search them and know their hearts, try them and know their thoughts. They ask God to

Stepping into Destiny!

see if there is any wickedness in them and to lead them down the right path. It was Satan's purpose to bring about an eternal separation between God and man; but in Christ, we become more closely united to God than if we had never fallen. We rededicate ourselves back to God in mind, body and spirit.

RENEW

After your storm has passed over, you have come out of the wilderness, the fire has purified you, the trials and tribulations have made you stronger, and after the Lord has increased your faith in Him, you become renewed. More weight of God's glory rests upon you and divine favor is upon your life. You are no longer the person you use to be. Old things are passed away and all things have become new. God has given you a new heart and a new mind. The anointing upon your life has compelled many to you and you are yielding great fruit that is satisfying and refreshing to all who partake of it. Your Christian walk has been revitalized. It is no longer stale, but active, energetic and spiritually fulfilling. We all need to be renewed at some point in our Christian walk. Your renewal has caused your very presence to change the atmosphere wherever you go. When you enter a room, you change the atmosphere because of the light of God's glory in you! You are now an atmosphere changer. When you walk into a place, the peace and light of God within you permeates the environment. Your walk with the Lord has been renewed and it is a deeper, more fulfilling and closer relationship. Renewal is invigorating, refreshing and liberating.

FAITH

The Christian walk is a faith walk and it is not always easy. True faith is of the heart, not of the mind. God dwells in the heart, not the mind. What you think about in your mind drops to your heart. Once it gets in the heart, it passes over to the subconscious mind, which becomes part of your spirit. What is in the heart, changes who you are. It changes your personality, your behavior, and your thinking - for good or bad. A holy and self-denying life is the result of faith, not the grounds of it. The grace of God in Christ is the foundation for our hope, and that grace will be manifested in a life of obedience. Man says, "Show me and I'll trust you" but God says, "Trust me and I'll show you." That's faith. Are you trusting God without seeing any signs of deliverance in the natural realm? Faith is substance. Faith will bring the invisible substance into visible form. Got faith? We oftentimes do not understand why God allows certain things to happen in our lives and we get frustrated trying to figure it out. We wonder why we must struggle, we get mad with God and feel the discouragement of worry, doubt and fear; but as His children, rooted and grounded in Christ, we continue to hold on to His promises because we know that weeping may endure for a night, but joy comes in the morning. When you have a strong foundation (Christ), nothing, no one, and no circumstance will shake your faith because you know that God sits on the throne and is still working things out for your good. When you are planted by the Lord, you will be able to withstand the violent storms of life without becoming uprooted. He tries our faith so that we can try His faithfulness. The faith that you have in God, in His power, and in His promises should supersede every negative situation that presents itself to you. No matter what the situation may look like or what people may say, you must know with all your heart that if you are a child of God, then ALL things are working together for your good. Not SOME things but ALL things. Faith decides divine timing. How you deal with your test depends upon your faith in God to know that He will bring you out. That's the time to pray and exercise the faith that you say you have.

Faith is like a toothbrush, everybody should have one and use it daily, but they should not try to use someone else's. Faith is not like gasoline which runs out as you use it, but like a muscle, which grows stronger as you exercise it. Faith is believing in things that you cannot see with the natural eye, knowing that you shall soon see it. Faith is the substance of things hoped for, the evidence of things not seen (Hebrews 11:1). It is time to walk your faith out. Stop just having faith and begin walking in faith. You are there. You have arrived. All you have to do now is walk into it. Always affirm your desires in the present tense. The Bible says, "NOW" faith is the substance of things hoped for... Let the weak say, I AM strong. Let the poor say, I AM rich. Let the sick say, I AM healed. Why? Because you do not need to confess your weakness in your humanity, rather confess your strength in divinity. You are not becoming, you are. You are not "going to be" rich, healed, delivered, you already are! Thank God NOW for the victory. Praise Him NOW for what you already are. Many people do not understand this powerful principle, but it activates miracles. Only God can move mountains, but faith and prayer can move God.

DELAYED BUT NOT DENIED

The Word that God has spoken over your life will come to pass. It may be delayed, but will not be denied. If more Christians today could receive more sermons on the depths, destruction and devastation of sin, they would not be repeating the same tests over and over. Judgment must begin at the house of God. Unfortunately, many sermons preached today are deliberately safe and soothing to the ears. These popular sermon topics deal with prosperity, promotion, obtaining wealth, favor, blessings, walking in the overflow, mentioning your "haters" and are preached without teaching the necessary requirements that must be adhered to before those blessings can manifest. Virtues such as holiness, humility, piety, self-denial, integrity and keeping the commandments are rarely taught and if touched on, are so scarcely mentioned that they will be missed if one blinks. Unfortunately, the desire to retain membership and increase numbers in the congregation supersedes the responsibility to teach the whole Word of God without partiality. Some spiritual leaders are too concerned about growing numbers and are rarely concerned about growing the people. Many modern pastors of the day are afraid to "offend" anyone. As a result of their willful refusal to teach the uncompromised Word of God, sin, vice, homosexuality, bribery, adultery, fornication, gossip, lies, deceit, backstabbing, and betrayal pervades many churches of the present day. This sickness starts from the head and spreads throughout the body of Christ. The whole body becomes sick, but they know it not because they love what the world loves. Counterfeit holiness is still doing its work of deception diverting minds from the scriptures and leading the people of God to follow their own feelings and passions rather than to yield obedience to the Word of God in scripture. Ichabod! Ichabod! Ichabod! meaning, *The glory of God has departed* is heard in the ears of those who can hear in the Spirit. The churches of today have become business organizations rather than spiritual hospitals. When we cease being a family and become an organization, we have ceased to be a true church.

Families are built by relationships not organizations. Programs, conferences, revivals and church and pastor's anniversaries, continue being held while the life of the Spirit of God has departed. Whatever is built upon the authority of man will be overthrown, but that which is founded upon the Rock of God's immutable Word shall stand forever. Are the traditions of men more worthy of faith than the gospel of our Savior? Where does that leave the people of God? Clinging to dead religion, that's where! Their walk and purpose is stifled due to neglect of being properly fed. They get junk food for the soul and amusement for the flesh week after week instead of a powerful, life-giving Word that will effect change in their lives. We are so busy feeding our flesh that our spirit is dying. Many of the members in these particular churches have religion, but not relationship. Because of this, their God is the pastor. They know no other God because they have not been taught how to get to know the true and Living God through the study of the Word and prayer. Their knowledge of God goes no farther than what they get from the pastor in church. Their prayers go no farther than what the pastor prays. They receive very little if any light and therefore walk in darkness. Satan seeks to divert believers' thoughts and affections from God and fix them upon human agencies. He leads them to honor the mere instrument and to ignore the Hand who directs all the events of providence. The people of God are directed to the scriptures as their safeguard against the influence of false teachers and the delusive power of spirits of darkness. The promises of God for their life are delayed because they are not receiving an in-season, on time, present truth Word that will catapult them to the next spiritual level. They go around and around the same mountain of trial and it is not until they either move from under dead religion or begin to absorb themselves in the Word of God and prayer that they discover God's purpose for their lives.

DIVINE FAVOR

The favor of God upon your life does not mean that you will not face disappointments, betrayal or have problems. It simply means that as you go through those things, there is a greater degree of mercy and grace upon you. With God's favor, He goes before you and touches the hearts and minds of the people you will encounter. When the favor of God is upon your life, He will whisper your name into the ears of the right people and speak your name out of the mouths of the right people. The bottom line is this: You always come out on top with God's favor in your life.

    The favor of God was with Joseph although he was still thrown in a pit and left for dead, but favor did not allow him to die. The favor of God did not stop Joseph from going to jail, but he had favor while in there. God's favor did not stop the three Hebrew boys from being thrown in the fiery furnace, but favor did not allow them to burn. God's favor did not stop Daniel from going into the lion's den, but favor did not allow him to be eaten up. God's favor may not stop your court date, but his favor will be with you in court. It may not stop the foreclosure process, but favor will allow you to remain in the home. It may not stop the surgery, but favor will see that it is successful. My point is that God allows us to go through things so that we will continue to trust Him, even though it may be the 12th hour; but if you trust Him, His favor will guarantee that the situation will work out for your good. Everyone does not have God's favor. Do you?

THE GREATNESS WITHIN YOU

    Many can feel something great on the inside of them, but do not know how to release that greatness. Some do know how, but are looking for a shortcut because the pleasures of this world have them too attached. They do not want to give up the pleasures of this world in exchange for what God has for them. You must be willing to give up something in exchange for something better. Something has to be sacrificed. In order for a tree to come forth, a seed must first die. In order for gold to be purified, it must first go through the fire. To produce the wine, the grapes must be crushed, to produce the oil the olives must be pressed, to produce greatness in you, you must give up something. Everything comes with a cost. There is no way around it. What are you willing to give up in order to go higher? There are no shortcuts to the anointing. Many have tried, but after years of running, looking for shortcuts, taking the broad and wide path, sitting under wrong teaching and trying to do things their own way, they eventually end up doing it God's way. Decades may have passed, opportunities lost and many tears shed, but eventually, their greatness comes forth - God's way. God does not compromise. The promise was delayed, but not denied.

PRESENT TRUTH

You shall know the truth and the truth shall make you free (John 8:32). In order to get free, you must know the truth and become established in *present* truth. Every Word written between the pages of the sacred scriptures is the truth, the inspired Word of God. This Word of truth has been preserved uncorrupted throughout all the ages of darkness. It bore not the stamp of men, but the impression of God. The Holy Scriptures contain treasures of truth that are revealed only to the earnest, most prayerful seeker. We must continuously search the scriptures for truth as hid treasures. As you study the Word of God with a pure heart and love for the truth, angels of heaven will be by your side and rays of light will shine from heaven and reveal the treasures of truth to your understanding. There is a present truth for this time, but you can only discover what it is by diligently, earnestly and consistently studying the scriptures. We must always be ready to speak the present mind of Christ for each situation. There is nothing like an "ON TIME" word. There is a time and season for all things to be released out of the mouth. When the man or woman of God is "in tune" to what the Spirit is saying in the present day, the Word will penetrates the hearts and minds of the sheep of God and speak to their specific situation. One may say something to another that may very well be true, but because the timing is not right, the person does not receive their words, neither do they not receive the person who spoke them. With wisdom and discernment, we know WHAT to say and WHEN to say it.

We must study the Word of God with an intensity of interest. It is not the most talented, but the most humble and devoted who God speaks to and through. Those who desire to please the Father more than they desire to please man will speak the present mind of Christ as it is impressed upon them by the Holy Spirit. God is a God of order and will operate decently and in order through His messengers. In order to speak what 'Thus saith the Lord' you must have boldness. God has not called the weak in this present day. He has called the bold and radical warriors who will speak the present truth during this present time in boldness. *And now, Lord, behold their threatenings: and grant unto thy servants, that with all **boldness** they may speak thy word, By stretching forth thine hand to heal; and that signs and wonders may be done by the name of thy holy child Jesus. And when they had prayed, the place was shaken where they were assembled together; and they were all filled with the Holy Ghost, and they spoke the word of God with **boldness** (Acts 4:29-31).* Let us pray for boldness in this present day!

CHAPTER ENDING WISDOM KEYS

- ♦ You do not have to confess your weakness in your humanity, but rather declare your strength, which is in divinity.

- ♦ Christ was treated as we deserve so that we could be treated as He deserves. He was condemned for our sins, in which He had no share, so that we could be justified by His righteousness, in which we had no share.

- There is a present truth for this time, but you can only discover what it is by diligently, earnestly and consistently studying the scriptures.

- The Holy Scriptures contain treasures of truth that are revealed only to the earnest, most prayerful seeker. We must continuously search the scriptures for truth as hid treasures.

- You must be willing to give up something in exchange for something better. Something has to be sacrificed. In order for a tree to come forth, a seed must first die. In order for gold to be purified, it must first go through the fire.

Chapter 4
Spiritual Gifts

> *Having then gifts differing according to the grace that is given to us, whether prophecy, let us prophesy according to the proportion of faith; or ministry, let us wait on our ministering: or he that teaches, on teaching; or he that exhorts, on exhortation: he that gives, let him do it with simplicity; he that rules, with diligence; he that shows mercy, with cheerfulness*
> *(Romans 12:6-8).*

In chapter one, we discussed how each person is sent to this earth with a distinct purpose and at least one natural gift on the inside of them. Everyone is born with innate gifts and when those gifts are discovered and used, you begin unfolding your purpose. Proverbs 18:6 states that, *"Your gift shall make room for you"* which simply means that your gift can pave the way for you to obtain favor, mercy, prosperity, and even wealth. Your gift is connected to your purpose and is to be used in connection with it. Examples of natural gifts could be singing, dancing, cooking, writing poetry, drawing, sowing, baking, painting, book-writing, calculating numbers, decorating, planning events, organizing, leadership, encouraging, mechanics, technology, entrepreneurship, etc. There is a litany of gifts that men and women on the earth have inside of them and the variation of those gifts are infinite. With practice, your gifts become extraordinary and when used for God's glory, will advance the Kingdom mightily. However, there are also spiritual gifts that we are not born with, but obtain after we are "born again." Just as you are born of the flesh with a natural gift inside you, when you are "born again" you receive a spiritual motivational gift inside and there are no gifts as precious as God's spiritual gifts. The spiritual gifts are given by the Holy Spirit only and cannot be duplicated, replicated or imitated. It is needful that every believer uses their spiritual gifts *...for the perfecting of the saints, for the work of the ministry, for the edification of the body of Christ (Ephesians 4:8)*. In these last days, we need spiritual gifts in order to do the work of the ministry effectively and all gifts must work in harmony with each other.

MOTIVATIONAL GIFTS

There are seven motivational gifts outlined in Romans 12:6-8. Every believer has one dominating motivational gift, which is the driving force of everything they do. When acting from this motivational gift, you perform at your greatest potential, have the greatest sense of fulfillment, and are the most productive. You can have several ministry or manifestation gifts, but only one that dominates all others. Your motivational gift helps you to understand other people and yourself better. The seven motivational gifts are listed below. Definitions are not given because the words are plain in their meanings. Keep in mind that you only have one that dominates:

1. Exhorting
2. Giving
3. Ministry
4. Prophecy
5. Ruling
6. Showing Mercy
7. Teaching

Spiritual Gifts

These gifts characterize your basic motivations or inherent predispositions. Although you have one dominant gift, you may also have smaller mixtures of the other six. *Having then gifts differing according to the grace that is given to us, whether **prophecy**, let us prophesy according to the proportion of faith; or **ministry**, let us wait on our ministering: or he that **teaches**, on **teaching**; or he that **exhorts**, on exhortation: he that **gives**, let him do it with simplicity; he that **rules**, with diligence; he that **shows mercy**, with cheerfulness (Romans 12:6-8).*

THE 9 GIFTS COMPARED TO THE 9 FRUITS

Many Christians seek the Gifts of the Spirit without first acquiring and exemplifying the Fruit of the Spirit in their lives. We must have the Fruit of the Spirit at work in our lives first, if we want God to entrust us with the Gifts of the Spirit. Exemplifying the fruit of the Spirit is much more important to God than having His Gifts. Let us seek to display the Fruit of the Spirit first. Everything else follows suit.

Gifts of the Spirit	**Fruits of the Spirit**
1 Corinthians 12	Galatians 5:22-23
1. Word of Wisdom	1. Love
2. Word of Knowledge	2. Joy
3. Discerning of Spirits	3. Peace
4. Faith	4. Longsuffering
5. Healings	5. Gentleness
6. Miracles	6. Goodness
7. Prophecy	7. Faith
8. Divers Tongues	8. Meekness
9. Interpretation of Tongues	9. Temperance

NINE GIFTS OF THE HOLY SPIRIT

Just as we have five physical senses that allow us to function effectively in the natural realm, we also have nine gifts of the Holy Spirit that allow us to function effectively in the spiritual realm as one body. The main purpose of spiritual gifts is to manifest the supernatural goals of God. Spiritual gifts enable the people of God to mature in the things of God, edify others, and do the work of the ministry effectively. Every believer should be open to the working of these gifts in their lives in accordance with the scriptures. When spiritual gifts are displayed, it publicly confirms that you are a true believer and ambassador of God. This is one undeniable way that you are identified as a believer in Christ Jesus. God uses human agencies as instruments to bring about His purposes on earth. We, as humans are simply the conduits. For example, when God has a new song to be sung, He does not step down and sing it Himself. He drops the song into the spirits of many. The one who hears it in the spirit, embraces it quickly, writes it down and sings it, is the one used to bring about that purpose. When God has a message for His children, He does not speak audibly to them, He uses a prophet as His mouthpiece to bring His message forth; When God answers a prayer, He whispers His child's name into someone's ear and impresses upon them to bless that particular person in a specific way. When the messengers are obedient, God's purposes are carried out. That is the pattern of God. He uses men, women and children to carry out His purposes. With natural gifts, we carry out natural ambitions, but with spiritual gifts, we carry out spiritual plans. The Spirit accomplishes much more than the natural assignments.

The Spirit-filled experience is more than just speaking in tongues, but it is coming into the fullness of the plan of God for our lives. As with natural gifts, not everyone will have the same gift, but everyone is given a measure. *Now there are diversities of gifts, but the same Spirit. And there are differences of*

Spiritual Gifts

administrations, but the same Lord. And there are diversities of operations, but it is the same God which works all in all (1 Corinthians 12:4). The Holy Spirit is the dispenser of all Spiritual gifts to bring about integrity in worship and kingdom expression. As you see on page 47, there are nine gifts of the Holy Spirit to profit the body of the church. These gifts are available to EVERY believer as the Holy Spirit distributes them.

*For to one is given by the Spirit the **Word of wisdom**; to another the **Word of knowledge** by the same Spirit; to another **Faith** by the same Spirit; to another the **Gifts of healing** by the same Spirit; to another the **Working of miracles**; to another **Prophecy**; to another **Discerning of spirits**; to another **Divers kinds of tongues**; to another the **Interpretation of tongues**: But all these works that one and the selfsame Spirit, dividing to every man severally as he will (1 Corinthians 12).*

These nine gifts can be broken down into three categories:

        Revelation Gifts (gifts that reveal)
           Word of Wisdom
           Word of Knowledge
           Discerning of Spirits

        Power Gifts (gifts that show action)
           Faith
           Healing
           Miracles

        Inspiration Gifts (gifts that edify)
           Prophecy
           Divers Tongues
           Interpretation of Tongues

Word of Wisdom (Revelation Gift)
It was mentioned in chapter three that there are three types of wisdom: the wisdom of God (1 Corinthians 2:6-7); the wisdom of man (Ecclesiastes 1:16-18); and the wisdom of the world (1 Corinthians 2:6). The gift of the Word of Wisdom spoken here is given by the Holy Spirit and is the wisdom that comes from God. It is to supernaturally disclose the mind, purpose, and plan of God as applied to a specific future situation. It is to speak hidden truths of what is not known. This gift is the application of specific knowledge that can only come from God. It cannot be gained through study or research, but reveals prophetic future for accomplishing God's will in a given situation. To have the gift of Wisdom is to have [some of] the Wisdom of God. It is the undisputable, supernatural impartation of facts. It is received from God through asking in prayer. This gift works hand-in-hand with the other two revelation gifts, knowledge and discernment. The fruit of the Spirit that is present when this gift is being used is love.

Word of Knowledge (Revelation Gift)
This gift is a supernatural revelation of information about specific things transpiring in someone's life at the present time and has to do with an immediate need. It enables a person to understand the deeper matters of the gospel and comes in a mental image. It is supernatural insight of a situation, problem, circumstance or body of facts that the revealer had no prior knowledge of. A Word of knowledge is a conviction that comes in a similitude. When a Word of knowledge is given, it conveys the divine will and plan of God. This knowledge involves moral wisdom for right living and relationships. It refers to knowledge of God or of the things that belong to God, as related in the gospel.

Spiritual Gifts

In Mathew 10:19, Jesus told the apostles, *When they deliver you up, take no thought **how** or **what** ye shall speak: for it shall be given you in that same hour what ye shall speak.* The "how" in this scripture refers to the *Word of Wisdom* and the "what" in the scripture refers to the *Word of Knowledge.* The fruit of the Spirit that is present when this gift is being used is joy.

Discerning of Spirits (Revelation Gift)
Discerning of spirits is having spiritual insight to detect the true spirit behind the acts and manifestations taking place around us. This gift protects and guards the life of Christians. Being able to perceive the source of spiritual manifestation and determine whether or not it is God is having the gift of Discerning of Spirits. It is not criticizing, finding fault or being suspicious, rather it is simply calling out the spirit that is not of God. As with all the other gifts, only through the power of the Holy Ghost can this gift be executed. With this gift, one can detect the realm of the spirit and ascertain their activities. With this gift, one is given supernatural revelation and can detect the plans and purposes of the enemy and his forces. The fruit of the Spirit that is present when this gift is being used is temperance.

How to discern (test) a Spirit:
1. By their fruit. A good tree cannot bring forth corrupt fruit; neither can a corrupt tree bring forth good fruit. Watch conduct and actions. Listen to the nature of conversations.

2. Is Jesus Christ being exalted as the risen Savior and son of the Living God?

3. Listen to what is being preached/taught. Is it in line with scripture? All teaching must be tested by the oracles of God. The Word of God never changes.

Faith (Power Gift)
Having the gift of faith is having the constant, consistent, unwavering ability to believe God without doubt. These have spiritual vision. They look more at the unseen rather than how it looks in the natural. They meet adverse circumstances with trust in God's Words and His promises. This gift operates in miracles, healings, and in the realm of impossibilities. Faith produces miracles, but miracles do not necessarily produce faith. The Bible speaks of three different kinds of faith:

1. **Saving Faith** - This faith gets you into heaven.

2. **Fruit of Faith** - This Faith gets heaven into you.

3. **Gift of Faith** - Comes from having both saving faith and fruit of faith. This is having the unwavering ability to believe in the miraculous.

Saving Faith produces the active faith of the fruit of the Spirit which, in turn produces the gift of faith. When the gift of faith is empowered, the results are miraculous! The fruit of the Spirit that is present when this gift is being used is peace.

Healings (Power Gift)
The gift of healings refers to being totally cured or healed without human aid. This gift is needed for the cure of specific diseases and it can be prayed for, as with all the other gifts. Healing can come through the touch of faith simply by speaking the Word of faith or by the presence of God being manifested. The Bible speaks of gifts of healings because there are different types of healings:

1. Physical (diabetes, blindness, cancer, deafness, etc.)

2. Emotional (worry, depression, discouragement, heartbroken, etc.)

3. Spiritual (bitterness, unforgiveness, greed, guilt, shame, etc.)

This gift has many variations. While one person with this gift may be able to heal a person of cancer, another may be able to cure lower back problems or to heal someone from a root of bitterness. The fruit of the Spirit that is present when this gift is being used is longsuffering.

Miracles (Power Gift)
A miracle is a supernatural intervention from the normal course of events. It is a divine overriding of, or interference with, natural order. It can be described as the performance of something which is against the laws of nature or a supernatural power to intervene and counteract earthly and evil forces. The word "miracle" comes from the Greek word "dunamis", which means *power and might that multiplies itself.* This gift works very closely with the gift of faith and healings to bring authority over Satan, sickness, sin and the binding forces of this age.

Jesus said, *Ye do err, not knowing the scriptures, nor the power of God (Mathew 22:29)*. The Apostle Paul warned Timothy about those who have a "form" of Godliness, but deny the power thereof. If you want the gift of miracles to operate in you, then be sure that you have the Word of God in you. Miracles are the product of the spoken Word of God because the Word of God and God are one. Jesus performed many miracles because He had compassion on the crowds and acted with kindness. Therefore, the fruit of the Spirit that is present when this gift is being used is gentleness (kindness).

Prophecy (Inspiration Gift)
To prophecy means to foretell, proclaim, or deliver the truth directly from God. It is conveying in human words a message that God brings to the mind of the prophet. It is supernatural disclosure, a sudden Spirit inspired insight that brings exhortation to the body of Christ. Prophecy is a divinely inspired and anointed utterance; a supernatural proclamation from God in a known language. It comes from a manifestation of the Spirit of God in a place. Although intellect, faith, and will are used in this gift, it is not predicated upon intellect. The Spirit of God Himself impresses His message upon the mind of the messenger. The gift of prophecy operates when worship is high, other prophets are present, and there is laying on of hands by ministers. All who have the infilling of the Holy Spirit may possess the gift of prophecy. Prophecy is important to the body of Christ because not only does it edify and exhort, but it brings spiritual vision, revival and restoration to the people of God. It moves believers to their right position in Christ.

According to the scriptures, the gift of prophecy is the most important spiritual gift that we should desire because it edifies both the prophet and the church. Paul states, *I would that ye all spoke with tongues but rather that ye prophesied: for greater is he that prophesied than he that speaks with tongues, except he interpret, that the church may receive edifying (1 Corinthians 14: 4-5).* The subject of prophecy is still greatly misunderstood and even despised in certain places because it is difficult to grasp the concept that God actually speaks directly through humans; this makes many uncomfortable at the direct voice of God. The purpose of prophecy is to edify, exhort, comfort, build up and strengthen, and should always lead to the Word of God. God is in unison with Himself. He never speaks contrary to His written Word. The spirits of the prophets are subject to the prophets, therefore prophecy should be judged. There are seven ways to judge prophecy. If the message does not line up, then it is to be rejected. The seven ways to judge prophecy are:

1. By the fruit (Mathew 7:16-18-20)
2. Does the prophecy glorify Christ? (John 16:14:1 Corinthians 12:3; 1 John 4:1-2)
3. Is it in line with scripture? (Isaiah 8:20)
4. Do the prophecies come to pass? (Even though they may come to pass, does not mean they are of God. The test is whether the prophecy glorifies Jesus.)
5. Is the prophecy clear? (Isaiah 28:13) True prophecy is not confusing or disjointed.
6. Does the prophecy produce liberty? (True prophecy does not put you in bondage, rather it sets you free. (Romans 8:5)
7. Does your Spirit receive it? (True prophecies should witness to the spirit of all believers. (1 John 2:20, 27)

The fruit of the Spirit that is present when this gift is being used is goodness.

Divers Tongues (Inspiration Gift)
Divers tongues are a supernatural utterance in an unknown tongue. The gift of diver's tongues is for public ministry and is a gift from God to the church. Divers mean different tongues. With diver's tongues, the languages change from one to another. Songs can be sang using divers tongue as well. The fruit of the Spirit that is present when this gift is being used is also faith.

The gift of tongues is the *evidence* of the Holy Spirit in the life of a believer after they have been baptized. There is a difference between tongues and divers tongues. At Pentecost, the church received the gift to communicate the gospel in foreign languages. These tongues were "known" tongues. They were actual languages that had not been studied by the believer uttering them; nonetheless, they were known to those who were from the particular country where the language is spoken. During this time, the Holy Spirit came upon believers empowering them to witness and prophesy. *And they were all filled with the Holy Ghost, and began to speak with other tongues, as the Spirit gave them utterance. And there were dwelling at Jerusalem Jews, devout men, out of every nation under heaven. Now when this was noised abroad, the multitude came together, and were confounded, because every man heard them speak in his own language (Acts 2:4-6).* God has given every believer, through His Holy Spirit the gift to speak in a language we do not know by human means. God has given the promise to all who want to serve Him. In some countries believers speak in English, but do not know or have never studied English. This is tongues to them. There are three types of tongues mentioned in the sacred scriptures:

1. **An unknown tongue** (1 Corinthians 14:2).
   This type of tongue edifies you, assists you in prayer during personal prayer time, stirs up the prophetic ministry in you, refreshes your soul, gives victory over the devil, brings you into the presence of God, aids you in intercession, and helps you worship in the Spirit.

Spiritual Gifts

2. **A known tongue**
   This is a sign to unbelievers (1 Corinthians 14:2; Acts 2:6). This may be unknown to the one speaking, but known to people in a far away country.

3. **A interpreted tongue**
   This tongue is understood through interpretation and edifies the church.

Speaking in tongues serve two functions.
1. **Personal** - for your personal prayer life to build you up and help usher you into the gift of prophecy. (No interpretation is necessary when used in this manner.)

2. **Public** - a direct message in tongues followed by an interpretation. This is for the edification of the church and requires an interpreter.

Interpretation (Inspiration Gift)
After divers tongues have gone forth, one who has the gift of interpretation will rise up to give the supernatural verbalization to reveal the meaning of what has been uttered. This gift operates out of the mind of the Spirit rather than the mind of person. Interpretation is not the same thing as translation because the one interpreting does not understand the tongue that has gone forth. When one translates, he or she understands what is being said, and then puts the message in their own words, but with interpretation of tongues, the interpreter does not understand the tongues when they are being uttered. The Spirit has to reveal to them what has been said afterwards.

This gift of interpretation is the second of the three of the vocal gifts of the Holy Spirit. When combined with the inspirational gift of divers tongues, the miraculous and supernatural phenomenon of prophecy results. If someone addresses the body with divers tongues, you can pray and ask God to give you the interpretation so that others will understand what has been said. You can also ask the Lord to give you interpretation in your own prayer time so that you can understand what your spirit has spoken to Him. When you ask earnestly and wholeheartedly, the Lord will give you the gift of interpretation. The fruit of the Spirit that is present when this gift is being used is meekness.

As you now know, there are many spiritual gifts available for the believer to have in their Christian walk. These gifts can be yours for the asking. No particular gifts are exclusive to any group of people, but they are available to the believer who earnestly desires to have them. Spiritual gifts will aid you in your prayers, guide you in edifying the body of Christ, strengthen you when you need it and manifest through you in healing and encouraging others. Jesus Christ's last words to his disciples before He ascended to heaven were, *"Go ye into all the world, and preach the gospel to every creature. He that believeth and is baptized shall be saved; but he that believeth not shall be damned. And these signs shall follow them that believe; In my name shall they cast out devils; they shall speak with new tongues; They shall take up serpents; and if they drink any deadly thing, it shall not hurt them; they shall lay hands on the sick, and they shall recover.*" The believer's life should have some signs. If you are in a church where none of the above gifts are operating, then you may be in a dead church. It may just take you to bring the life back to it. The church may have a great preacher, a wonderful praise team, a phenomenal choir and awesome ministries, but do they encourage the use of spiritual gifts and do they do the following as evidenced by the above scripture?

Spiritual Gifts

1. cast out devils
2. speak with tongues
3. lay hands on the sick

Of course, I do not expect to see churches taking up serpents or drinking deadly things, but at the very least, do they teach about the gifts of the Spirit, specifically speaking in tongues or do they turn their noses up at it? Every Christian should speak in tongues. According to I Corinthians 14:5, when you speak in tongues you are building yourself up in the most holy faith. Since we know that speaking in tongues is available to all believers and builds us up in God, then we all should desire to have it. We need every blessing in Christ that is available to us in order to help strengthen us in the days in which we are living. The cost of the anointing is not cheap, but the rewards that come with it are extraordinary, powerful, and uniquely executed in the life of everyone who has paid for it. You rarely see, if ever a powerful man or woman of God who does not have any spiritual gifts. In order to break ground on the enemy's territory, you must have evidence that you are a child of God and be able to demonstrate the works of the Holy Spirit in your life. Your tests, trials, hardships and difficulties have earned you a powerful anointing and with that anointing comes spiritual gifts to help you in this Christian walk. By the strength and the power of the anointing that rests upon you, others can receive their spiritual gifts just by being in your presence. You will get to a point where you will be able to lay hands on a believer and command their gifts to come forth.

    It can sometimes be difficult for people to awaken and begin walking in their spiritual gifts when the spiritual gifts are not taught or demonstrated in their current place of worship. For this reason, it is imperative that you have a spiritual mentor who can deposit in you. When you are under the tutelage of one who carries a mantle, the spirit they walk in is often transferred to you and you pick up the spiritual gifts they have. You simply cannot be around someone without picking up their ways and sometimes even their skills. Just as Elisha received a double portion of Elijah's spirit, the same should happen when we are under the leadership of those whose spiritual gifts are actively displayed in their lives. If you hang with prophets long enough, you will eventually prophecy! I have never been to a church where the pastor speaks in tongues, but the congregation does not, nor have I been to a church where the pastor prophecies, but no one else in the church does. It is expected that whenever you find one prophet in a place, you will find two, three, or more because the prophets must judge the prophecies going forth. One will prophecy and the others will judge. That's proper heavenly protocol.

It is my opinion that every Christian should have a spiritual mentor who more mature than them in the spirit realm. This includes ministers and pastors alike. No one knows all they need to know. Anything without a head is abnormal. Everyone needs to have a spiritual head. There is always more learning that needs to take place and when we have someone who can meet us where we are, then take us higher, we are blessed indeed. Learn as much as you can under your mentor because the time will come when you will need to mentor someone else and you can only deposit in them what you have in you to deposit. If there is nothing worth learning in you or if all you have to offer is milk (a superficial word) then you won't have many followers and if you don't have anyone following you, then how can you be a leader? In order to be a good leader, you must first be a good follower and absorb all you can. Jesus was the greatest teacher/preacher/mentor there ever was. He taught his disciples by having them watch Him. They listened to how He taught, how He compassionately interacted with the people, how He dealt

Spiritual Gifts

with His enemies, how He laid hands, how He healed, how He addressed demons and how He responded as He was being crucified. After His ascension, they were able to effectively demonstrate all that they had learning under His training. The followers became leaders.

If you truly desire to operate in your spiritual gifts, but there is no one in your life who demonstrates these gifts, then pray and ask God to send you to someone. He will do it by way of His divine providence, but you have to have spiritual vision to recognize that person when you meet them. God will set up the divine appointment, but it is up to you to capitalize on it. God knows the desires of your heart and He will bless you with your Spiritual gifts if you truly desire to have them!

The baptism of the Holy Spirit is Biblical and cannot be explained away. Speaking in tongues is as real today as it was at Pentecost. The Scripture cannot be broken. If you are a born-again Christian, you have the Holy Spirit dwelling in you. If you desire to speak in tongues, and you believe from the book of Acts that you can have the same impartation they had, then simply ask the Lord Jesus for manifestation of the gift. Read Acts 2:1-15 and 1 Corinthians 14:5-15 and pray for the gift of speaking in tongues. After that, just open your mouth as you are praying and let the tongues flow up and out of your belly as rivers of living waters.

PRAYER FOR TONGUES

Heavenly Father, in Jesus' name, I humbly ask You to stir up the gift of tongues in me by the Power of your Holy Ghost. Remove all obstacles in the way of me receiving my gift. Allow me to use my tongues to communicate with you out of my spirit, refresh my soul, strengthen me, and to worship you in Spirit and in Truth. I thank you by faith for what you have already done. In the name of Jesus, I pray. Amen.

Now, thank and praise the Lord for what is already done in the Spirit. Allow the manifestation to come forth. Open your mouth and speak. Then obediently extend your expressions of love by praying and thanking Him in tongues.

CHAPTER ENDING WISDOM KEYS

- There are three *types* of gifts: motivation, ministry and manifestation and seven motivation gifts. Every believer has only one motivation gift, which is the driving force of everything you do.

- There are three types of wisdom: the wisdom of God (1 Corinthians 2:6-7); the wisdom of man (Ecclesiastes 1:16-18); and the wisdom of the world (1 Corinthians 2:6).

- If you want the gift of miracles to operate in you, then be sure that you have the Word of God in you. Miracles are the product of the spoken Word of God because the Word of God and God are one.

- According to the scriptures, the gift of prophecy is the most important spiritual gift that we should desire because it edifies the believer and it edifies the church.

- If you are a born-again Christian, you have the Holy Spirit dwelling in you. If you desire to speak in tongues, and you believe from the book of Acts that you can have the same impartation they had, then simply ask the Lord Jesus for the manifestation of the gift.

Chapter 5
The Prosperity Anointing

> *Beloved, I wish above all things that thou may prosper and be in health, even as thy soul prospers.*
> *(3 John 1:2-3)*

Every normal-thinking person has a desire to be prosperous, be that desire hidden or not. It is the inherent aspiration of most people to seek to live abundantly and to rise from the rut of living in lack, limitation, and from paycheck to paycheck. The majority of people equate prosperity with money, but money is simply a tool used to achieve things that we want to possess. The outgrowth of prosperity is not only identified in dollars and cents, but can also be seen in terms of health. Good health is wealth. Financial wealth is typically a signal that one has achieved the laws of prosperity, but having money does not necessarily mean that one is prosperous. A person could have inherited millions of dollars, but still have a poverty consciousness. Although they may have money and the symbols that reflect money (luxurious houses, expensive cars, fine clothes, jewelry, etc.), that does not mean that they are prosperous. Prosperity is a mindset and begins in the mind. Once the mind has been saturated in the understanding of the laws of prosperity, the embodiment of that revelation is manifested in the outward life. The laws of prosperity encompass much. In fact, I was so curious as to why only a small percentage of people in this world are exceptionally prosperous and the larger percentage are not, that I devoted time to studying the lives of those who have achieved noteworthy success and are considered prosperous. Subsequently, I wrote a book entitled 'Prosperity is Your Birthright' (2009). I felt that it was and still is necessary that we understand that it is not God's will for believers to be poor, miserable, and broke. It is the will of God that we walk in prosperity if we desire to have it. Not everyone desires prosperity; some are content with the little they have and are happy with that. But for those who are not content with having only a little, there are secrets that you must know. There are laws that pertain to prosperity that must be adhered to on the part of the one seeking to achieve and maintain prosperity to a notable degree. Prosperity is connected to spiritual laws and principles and it is essential to understand what those laws and principles are so that people will not be ignorant as to why they are constantly struggling. One of the most disheartening things for me to see is a powerful, anointed, earnest seeker of God who is broke and struggling financially. Their soul is wealthy, but their bank account is poor. God desires for us to be prosperous in both soul *and* bank account. *Beloved, I wish above all things that thou may prosper and be in good health, even as thy soul prospers (3 John 1:2-3).*

MONEY

For centuries, people without money have turned their noses up at the rich, as though being rich was a terrible sin. To some degree today, people still think that way towards the rich even though in their own heart of hearts, they wish they themselves were rich. You are in a much better position to be able to increase the kingdom of God with money than without it. You have a right to be rich, but God is not going to entrust you with thousands of dollars if you have not been faithful with hundreds and He definitely will not entrust you with millions if you have not been faithful with thousands. Many are asking for more when they have not been faithful over what they already have. They do not need more; they simply need to be better stewards over what they already have. Only with money can one be free and unrestricted to have things that are necessary to reach their highest potential. Regardless of what people say, not having money to pay bills and worrying about if the electricity, water, or telephone is going to be turned off does not produce peace; it produces worry. Not having money for food, clothes or shoes is not a good state of mind to be in. How can one be in peace if they are hungry, but have no money to buy food? How can one be in peace if their child is walking around in worn-out shoes too small for them, but there is no money to buy another pair? Worrying and peace do not harmonize. If you have worry, you cannot have peace. You cannot praise and worship God to the fullest if you have worry on your mind. Lack and limitation produces worry and this interferes with your unrestricted praise to the Lord.

    Fulfillment in life is being everything that you desire to be and you can only be what you desire to be by making effective use of possessions; but you can only posses things if you have enough money to buy them. When you do not have enough money to buy them, you cannot adequately fulfill nor live up to your potential. *Money answers all things (Ecclesiastes 10:19).* There are specific laws associated with acquiring money and if learned, obeyed and practiced, will magnetize avalanches of money to you. God desires that you have an abundant life because you can accomplish so much more for the kingdom of God and be able to bless the people of God with money than without it. The wealthy have certain patterns of thinking that draws money to them. Their minds are a magnet for money because they have the money consciousness. If people in your town, your city, your state and your country can become rich, then so can you. Regardless of what your bank account may look like in the natural, if you begin doing certain things in a certain way and cultivating certain thought patterns, you will begin to draw money to you as well. Ask largely. There are no limitations in God. The only limit there is, is the limit that you put on what you can receive.

No one is deprived because an opportunity passed them by or because someone stopped them from pursuing their heart's desire, or because there is not enough room for another rich person. There is always room for one more, but you must compel that room for yourself. Just as a seed multiples after being planted, life by living multiplies itself also. The desire for more money is really the desire to have greater fulfillment in life. Never look at what seems to be a lack or shortage in the natural, instead, fix your spiritual eye on the unlimited supply in divinity. Looking at things in the natural produces bondage, not freedom.

Prosperity is a mindset and is directly linked to strategic actions and patterns of thinking. These actions and patterns of thinking must be consistently executed out of self-discipline. At different seasons, the tide of opportunity sets in different directions according to the needs of the whole. When the tides advance, there is prosperity; when they recede, there is a recession. However, if the laws and principles of prosperity are still being implemented in one's life, the advancing and receding of the tides will not affect their prosperity because prosperity is a mindset. Below is a list of principles that prosperity is linked to. When strategically applied to one's life, these principles cannot fail to prove successful.

There is an anointing for prosperity and once you are able to tap into that anointing, you will never be in poverty or lack another day of your life. Just as you grow and are elevated in the knowledge and wisdom of Christ Jesus and are able to enter into the throne room through prayers, supplication and a humble heart,

The Prosperity Anointing

you can also enter into the spiritual realm where prosperity permeates. Once you enter the knowledge of how to pull prosperity down from the spiritual into the natural, you have found the secret. As with anything else, prayer can bring about the revelation of the prosperity anointing. There are laws and principles that you can begin applying in order to exude prosperity energy. This sends the signal out that you are a student who is willing to exert the time, energy, effort and sacrifices to tap into the prosperity realm. Some of these laws and principles will be delineated for you in the next few pages.

Mindset

Your prosperity anointing is linked to your mindset. To reverse your fortune is to reverse your thinking. Your life is shaped by the thoughts you think. Your thoughts attract people, circumstances and events to you. You act according to what you are thinking. Your actions and your thinking are always in harmony with each other. Therefore, if you are thinking positive, happy, prosperous thoughts, your behavior will be pleasant, happy and joyful. Things and people that make up those exact thought elements will be drawn to you because like attracts like. On the contrary, if your thoughts are negative, self-deprecating, and focused upon the worse, then your behavior will be negative and self-deprecating. The situation will become bigger because you are sending out the thought magnet that will draw elements of the same nature of thoughts that you are thinking. Your mind must be trained to dismiss anything that enters it that you do not wish to see manifested in the natural. A prosperous mind focuses upon all that is good, affluent, beautiful and radiant, regardless of what things look like from the natural perspective. A prosperous mind is optimistic, positive, confident and always hopeful. This mind travels the road to success and understands that poverty and prosperity travel in two distinctly opposite directions.

Connecting yourself with people on a higher mental, intellectual, financial and/or spiritual realm will help expand your mindset and raise you up to the level where they are. You cannot get to the millionaire level with a hundred dollar mindset; you cannot get to the apostle level with a pastor's mindset; you cannot be on the Board of Directors with a blue collar mindset and you cannot get to the place where you are being chauffeured around if you are still on the bus stop. There is a great benefit in sitting under the tutelage of the great. If you hang with prophets, you will eventually prophecy. If you have millionaires as friends, it's because you are on your way to becoming one. The people you hang around will help to expand your mindset – or not.

A prosperous mind is a guarded mind. This mind always has a watchman at the mind gate ready to turn away negativity and worry. If a negative thought just happens to sneak in, a prosperous mind will detect it and evict it immediately. A prosperous mind is a strong mind that attracts and magnetizes all that is good and this is reflected in the personality and outward life. We are only given one life and when we begin to realize that our thought, imaginations and meditations shape our lives, circumstances and conditions, we will be very careful of what we entertain when thinking. You are where you are because your thinking has brought you there. Where will your thoughts today take you tomorrow? Be positive. Think positive. Act positive. Your mind creates your circumstances. *Finally, brethren, whatsoever things are true, whatsoever things are honest, whatsoever things are just, whatsoever things are pure, whatsoever things are lovely, whatsoever things are of good report; if there be any virtue, and if there be any praise,* **think** *on these things (Philippians 4:8).*

Meditation

Your prosperity anointing is linked to your meditation. Meditation brings about revelation. Many believers have developed an aversion towards the practice of meditation because of their personal prejudices against other religions that practice it. Meditation is essential when it comes to giving life to your highest dreams. It gives life to your visions. A vision can be broad at first, but an imagination makes it detailed and meditation gives it form and life. When you become proficient in meditation, you will begin to feel the embodiment of the things desired. No one ever receives anything good in life unless they first *imagine* it and *feel* it. When you begin to feel it, the focus has been transferred from your conscious mind to your subconscious mind and from there, it is just a matter of time before the ideal becomes the real.

Your outcome will not change until your focus changes. Meditation is the chief way to become successful in every area of your life. Change will not happen until you get an image of something new. In order to change your life, change what you picture in your mind. Change your imagination. What you focus on the longest becomes the strongest. You have in your life right now everything that you focused on long enough. If you are constantly facing the same problem, it is because you have not changed your focus. What are you constantly focusing on? When you focus on it long enough, it becomes meditation. Demand inwardly that a change in your life will happen. When you do that, you will begin to imagine a totally different world, one that reflects the express image of how you desire things to be from your inward perspective. Then, meditate upon that. Every great leader uses his or her imagination in order to create something out of a realm that is void of form. Imagination gives the blueprint and meditation gives the form.

Whatever you cannot see, you cannot have. If you cannot see it, you will not receive it. If you do not believe it, you will not achieve it. Jesus meditated. You can become one who meditates as well. True prayer is meditation. God favors silence and moves in that silence. The most powerful forces in the world are invisible: electricity, wind, radio waves, etc. Your most powerful forces are invisible too: your thoughts, meditation, imagination, love, ambition, perseverance, etc. These forces are silent, unseen and unfelt. But when you tap into the power that you already have and activate that power through meditation, it takes you to great heights of achievement. Everything you need is already within you. You must go within. If the Word of God is going to truly work in your life, then you must make the quality decision to meditate on the Word day and night. Meditation is a daily practice, a lifestyle. Do it until it becomes a part of you. In order to get something new, you must think something new, imagine something new, and meditate on something new. When you begin to meditate, you become focused on higher purposes. It is in meditation that you truly find out who you are. You come face to face with the real you in meditation.

You must be strategic with your meditation time. It must be designated. If you meditate on your aspirations at the wrong times, you steal energy and focus that needs to be put towards the present. You cannot work in a spirit of excellence with a divided mind. You cannot effectively perform in the present with your mind on the future. In order to rise from mediocre to good and from good to great, you must do things in a spirit of excellence at all times. For this reason, time should be designated for meditation on the ideal, but the duties of the current day must be fulfilled in a spirit of excellence in that day.

Self-discipline

Your prosperity anointing is linked to your self-discipline. Most people are mentally lazy and therefore allow their minds to think whatever it clings to. Prosperous people overcome mental laziness and the love of ease. A self-disciplined mind is a strong mind that exerts energy towards a positive end. Self-discipline requires sacrifice and self-denial. Prayer requires self-discipline; so does study, research, balancing a checkbook, exercising, reading, paying attention, practicing, cleaning up, etc. Prosperous people take the time to do things that mentally lazy people do not do. While mentally lazy people are wasting hours watching useless television shows, the self-disciplined person is using those same hours praying, fasting, studying the scriptures, developing a business plan, writing a book, researching information in their field, working on their website, making business phone calls, or exercising. The prosperous life is a disciplined life. Self-discipline will ripen your understanding and arouse an activity of mind and a keenness of perception that will prepare you for the vicissitudes of life. Most people live in mediocrity or below because they are too mentally lazy to put forth the effort necessary to find the road out of lack and limitation and travel it. What in your life can you give up in replace of something that is going to bring you closer to your goal of prosperity? *Go to the ant, thou sluggard; consider her ways, and be wise: which having no guide, overseer, or ruler, provides her meat in the summer, and gathers her food in the harvest (Proverbs 6:6-8).*

Giving

Your prosperity anointing is linked to your giving. Every time you give, you are sowing a seed. When God blesses you, those blessings are not for you only. Your blessings are to be shared with others. God has given each of us two hands for a reason, one hand to give and the other to receive. There must be a constant inflow and outgoing. You will never hold on to anything for long if you hoard them. If you tied a rope around your leg, circulation would be cut off after a while and your leg would die. It is the same with things. If there is no circulation, there is no flow. There must be a back and forth flow of going out and coming back in. Life is about giving and receiving. When God speaks to your spirit about sowing a seed, it is because He has a harvest on His mind for you! There can be no one-way flow. The mysterious part about giving is that the seed you sow never leaves your life. It only leaves your hand temporarily then goes into your future where it multiplies. When you release what you have, God will release what He has into your life. When you release what is in your hand, God releases what is in His hand. In order for anything to leave heaven, something must first leave the earth. If you refuse to give, then the amount you have will be the most it will ever be, but if you sow it, that will be the least it will ever be.

Never give with the expectation of being paid back. God pays you back in *due season*. When you give and expect it to be repaid, then do not expect God to also give to you. You have already been repaid; but if you give with an expectation that God will bless you, then nothing will compare to what He gives in return for your faithfulness. Prosperous people sow seeds and they give generously! *Give, and it shall be given unto you; good measure, pressed down, and shaken together, and running over, shall men give into your bosom. For with the same measure that ye mete withal it shall be measured to you again (Luke 6:38-39).*

Friends/Associations
Friends/associations
Your prosperity is linked to your friends and associations. You must be watchful of the people you choose to spend time with and allow into your inner circle. Your associations can help or hinder

you. They will either enhance or decease your image and credibility. Bad associations do corrupt good character. Take an inventory of who's around you. People come into your life to add, subtract, multiply or divide. Are your friends adding to your life? subtracting? multiplying? or dividing? Review those in your life to make sure they are adding to you as a person, not subtracting from your strength and vigor. The wrong people will hold you back, bring you drama, drag you down, and drain you of your creative energy. People come into your life as an appointment or a dis-appointment. Are your friends an appointment or disappointment? You can only move forward with the right people around you. Acquaint yourself with people who have already achieved what you are trying to achieve. If you hang with eagles, you will learn to fly high. Do you ever see black birds mixed with white birds? How about eagles with jay birds? What about chickens mixing with pigeons? How about ducks and roosters hanging out together? Whenever you see birds conjugating, they are always of the same feather. And so it is with humans. We mix with those we are like. Like attracts like in everything.

Great people hang around great people, do great things and exude great confidence. You become like those you interact with the most. Those who do not increase you will eventually decrease you. It is better to be alone than in the wrong company. You are wise when you learn and practice this truth. Some of your friends and acquaintances are fine for where you are now, but not for where you are going. As you rise to a new level of anointing and into another dimension of spirituality, some cannot go with you. In order to gain some things, you must give up some things. However, the space left behind by them will be filled with a new set of people that will help propel you and maintain you for where God is taking you. Get ready. It's going to happen, but watch your associations! *Be not deceived: evil communications corrupt good manners (1 Corinthians 15:33-34).*

Conversation
Your prosperity anointing is linked to your conversations. You attract what you talk about. God runs this universe through conversations between people. You may just be one conversation away from your breakthrough, but if you are too high and mighty to hold a conversation with someone you feel is beneath you, you may just miss out on a blessing. You cannot work hard enough for what you want on your own. At some point, you will need divine favor and you may never know who that favor will come through. It could be the person you least expect. When you change the nature of your conversation, you change your conditions, your mindset and your reality. The more specific you are when speaking, the quicker the manifestation will be and the more powerful the materialization.

You decree things in your life one word at a time and with strong convictions. Powerful statements produce powerful results. There is power in your words that go out into the universe and attracts the elements that are needed in order for prosperity to appear. The words used in your conversation do return to you for better or for worse. Who you are and what you think or feel is always revealed in your conversations. Nobody knows the quality of your mind until you open your mouth. Your daily conversations reveal what you think about, what you believe in, what you agree with and attract certain things and people to you. Your life is shaped by the words you speak. Be strategic in your conversations. Use affirmative words and eradicate negative, self-defeating, doubtful words out of your conversations. Exude energy, light, encouragement, confidence and optimism in your conversations with people. *Death and life are in the power of the tongue: and they that love it shall eat the fruit thereof (Proverbs*

18:21). People come into your life as an appointment or a disappointment.

Are your friends an appointment or disappointment? You can only move forward with the right people around you. Acquaint yourself with people who have already achieved what you are trying to achieve. If you hang with eagles, you will learn to fly high. Do you ever see black birds mixed with white birds? How about eagles with jay birds? What about chickens mixing with pigeons? How about ducks and roosters hanging out together? Whenever you see birds conjugating, they are always of the same feather. And so it is with humans. We mix with those we are like. Like attracts like in everything. *Be not deceived: evil communications corrupt good manners (1 Corinthians 15:33-34)*.

Self-confidence.

Your prosperity is linked to your self-confidence. People with self-confidence are inner-directed and self-assured. Their validation is not a function of people liking them or treating them well. They are validated from within and pursue their goals with the assurance and faith that they will beat all odds and overcome any obstacles. You gain self-confidence through self-reliance. When you begin to open your mind to greater possibilities for yourself, your consciousness begins to expand and you are then opened to seeing the truth of who you deeply are. False beliefs are automatically removed and replaced with beliefs that you know to be real and are willing to accept as truth. With self-confidence, you draw a different caliber of people to you. You begin to feel good about yourself and your thinking process changes for the better. Your confidence begins to draw positive situations and people to you and you accomplish goals that you thought were only a far-distant dream. Practice confidence and your fears and insecurities will soon vanish.

Gratitude

Your prosperity anointing is linked to your gratitude. Gratitude unlocks the door to the fullness of life. It turns what you have into more than enough. Gratitude turns denial into acceptance, chaos into order and confusion into clarity. It can turn a meal into a feast, a house into a home, and a stranger into a friend. Gratitude makes sense of your past and brings peace for today, while creating a vision for tomorrow. When you give thanks for what you already have, you open a floodgate of blessings that begin moving in your direction. Gratitude places you on a current that draws more your way. There is always something to be grateful for. I once read the following quote stated by Buddha, which sums up for me that there is always something to be grateful for: *"Let us rise up and be thankful, for if we did not learn a lot today, at least we learned a little, and if we did not learn a little, at least we didn't get sick, and if we got sick, at least we did not die, so let us still be thankful."* Through gratitude, your hands will begin to touch, feel, and experience the manifestation of things desired. Begin to feel the spirit of gratitude now. Be grateful for your many blessings. Your strong thankful emotion will draw your prosperity to you speedily. If your gratitude is strong and constant, God's reaction to you will be strong and continuous. It is gratitude that keeps you close to God. Faith is born of gratitude. *Enter into His gates with thanksgiving, and into His courts with praise: be thankful unto Him, and bless His name (Psalm 100:4)*

Actions

Your prosperity anointing is linked to your efficient and productive actions. Regardless of how much faith you have and how earnestly you have put all of the other principles to work in your life, if there is no action on your part, then everything you have done is in vain. No matter how positive you think, you must supplement your thinking with action. Your thoughts and actions must be in constant harmony. You must "do" something every day that will bring you closer to the vision that you are holding in your mind. It is written in the Word that, *Faith without works is dead (James 2:20)*. By thought, the image of what you want is given to you, but by action it is received. Hold the vision of your future aspirations before you always until it manifests, but act always in the present. You must know how to compartmentalize well. Meditate on what you desire to have, but work with excellence on what you currently have. Make room for what is coming, but treat what is already there with gratitude.

You cannot act with a divided mind: working in the present with your mind on the future. If you act with a divided mind, then you are not working on the present in a spirit of excellence. You can only be great by being larger than your presence space; but if you leave the work undone in your present space, then you are not larger than your present place. The progress of the world is stifled by those who do not complete the work in their present space. How can the world advance if everyone was smaller than their present space? It is the successful days that bring you to greatness. If your actions each day are successful, then you cannot fail to obtain prosperity. Your neglect or failure to complete a small action today could delay you in years of reaching your highest dream. You must first have a prosperity mindset. Set your goals, make your plans, work hard, sacrifice, toil, labor, and then be patient. If you are not willing to do those, then do not be envious of those who do and are experiencing the successful fruit of their hard work, labor and sacrifice. You can become quite successful without formal education, influential friends or even significant seed capital, but you will never be successful with weak faith, lack of planning and poor work habits. Success, prosperity and wealth are not going to just appear into your life. You must put in the work. Even so faith, if it hath not works, is dead, being alone. *Yea, a man may say, Thou hast faith, and I have works: show me thy faith without thy works, and I will show thee my faith by my works (James 2:17-18).*

Recognition

Your prosperity anointing is linked to your awareness and ability to recognize. Too many have sight, but no vision. Too many have eyes, but cannot see. Learn to discern. The ability to recognize can raise you from the rut of mediocrity and place you on the mountain of greatness. Open your eyes and see! Recognition can mean the same thing as discernment. Ask the Lord for clear vision to be able to recognize opportunities, money-making ideas, distractions, blessings, and quality people. Anything valuable in your life that you fail to recognize will not be celebrated. If it is not celebrated, it will not be rewarded, if it is not rewarded, then it will leave. We tend to look at people and sometimes wonder what "breaks" they had in life. We often fail to realize that people make their own breaks when they place themselves in positions to receive them. Breaks often come when you recognize opportunities and take hold of them quickly. If you fail to recognize what is before you, you may miss out on a great blessing. *Having eyes, see ye not? and having ears, hear ye not? (Mark 8:18)*

Recognition of Opportunities

The ability to recognize is a valuable asset. Opportunities come a dime a dozen, but there are some opportunities that have your name specifically stamped on them. Those are designed to be the key to your greatest prosperity. You must be able to discern which opportunity is worth pursuing and which is not. If you venture into every opportunity that comes your way, then you will waste a lot of time and money. Ask the Lord for an eagle's eye so that you will know what to pursue and what not to pursue. One of the saddest things in the world is for someone not to be able to recognize opportunity when it is presented to them, only to find out later that those who stayed for the long haul became millionaires. I read the story of those who were part of the original group exploring the "Google" concept. There were some who could not see the vision and abandoned the idea. However, today Google is the number one internet search engine in the world. The company profited 37.9 billion dollars in revenue in 2011. As of this writing (October 2012), their stocks closed at $754.83 per share on both the New York Stock Exchange and NASDAQ. Those who could not see the vision in the beginning missed out on the immense financial reward in the end. Some people may start out with you in the beginning, but if it is not in the plan for them to remain, eventually they will eliminate themselves along the way. I heard similar stories about Facebook and other powerful companies. When people want to leave, let them leave. Not everyone will be able to see the vision. Just pray that you can.

Recognition of Money-making Ideas

In the B-clause of Ecclesiastes 10:19, it is written that, *"Money answers all things."* Money comes from ideas. The blessings of the Lord are very rarely material. His blessings are first intangible: a sound mind, peace, joy, love and *ideas*. When God blesses you, He does not always give you the thing you desire. He often gives you the *idea* to get the thing desired. With implemented ideas, you can accomplish much more than the one limited thing you may be asking for. The principle is similar to the popular adage: *Give a man a fish and he will eat for a day, but teach him how to fish and he will eat for a lifetime.* If God gives you the one tangible thing you are asking for, then the blessing stops there, but if He impresses upon you an idea whereby you can accomplish that thing and much more, then He has deposited something much more beneficial and valuable inside you. Open your mind to create wealth-begetting ideas. Houses, cars and money are only byproducts of implementing the ideas that God gives you. The blessing is the *idea* and the ability to bring life to it, not the house, the money or the car. There are no cars or money in heaven.

Success, prosperity and wealth are not going to just appear on your doorstep. Many people start things and never finish any of them. You must plan the work and work the plan. They have so many scattered projects. Great people finish what they start no matter how big or small it is. When you begin to implement an idea, see it all the way through. That is the only way you will get the reward. *"If a task is once begun, never leave it til it's done; be the labor great or small, do it well or not at all" (author unknown).* Finish what you start and you will feel a great sense of accomplishment. When you are faithful with a few things, God will bless you with more!

Recognition of Quality people

God's all-seeing eye reads the hearts. He is the searcher of the hearts. He does not look at the outward appearance. He looks at the heart. He does not decide who to place His most valuable treasures into based upon how gorgeous or handsome people are. If we only judge people based upon their appearance, we can miss the message that God wants to give us through them. Some of God's most valuable treasures, gifts, and talents are found right within those whose outward appearance is not appealing to the natural eye. There are millionaires who look like beggars and there are those who look like millionaires and barely have money for gas. We must begin to see each other through the eyes of the spirit.

Jesus' coming had been foretold in prophecy through many messengers. However, when He arrived, the Jews did not "recognize" Him because they were looking with natural eyes. *...he hath no form nor comeliness; and when we shall see him, there is no beauty that we should desire him. He is despised and rejected of men; a man of sorrows, and acquainted with grief: and we hid as it were our faces from him; He was despised, and we esteemed Him not (Isaiah 53:2-3).* His glory was veiled so that the majesty of His outward form would not become an object of attraction. He shunned all outward display. Jesus purposed that no attraction of an earthly nature would call the people to His side. Only the beauty of heaven's truth would draw those who would follow Him. The character of the Messiah had long been foretold in prophecy, and He desired people to accept Him upon the testimony of the Word of God. Those who saw Him with the eyes of the Spirit received Him.

Both Absalom and Solomon had the same father, King David. One recognized his father's greatness but the other did not and tried to kill him. Both John the Baptist and Judas Iscariot had the same mentor, Jesus. One recognized Him as the Christ, but the other did not and betrayed Him. It is time for us to begin looking at each other through the eyes of the spirit so that we can "recognize" a God-sent when it comes into our lives.

Recognition of Divine Appointments

A divine appointment is a meeting with another person that has been ordered by God. In order to recognize a divine appointment, you must have your spiritual radar on and be able to see through the eyes of the spirit. Some have met their God-given mate through a divine appointment. Some met good friends through divine appointments. These "appointments" have been supernaturally scheduled to help both people in some way. We meet people who we teach and those we learn from.

The following story represents a divine appointment that happened in my life. There are a few others that I can think of, but this one stands out the most in my mind. It was the day of the 2012 presidential election between Barack Obama and Mitt Romney. My son and I were riding in the car and talking. All of a sudden, I pulled over to the side of the road. Stephan says, *Mom, why did you pull over?* I sat there and couldn't say a word because I had no idea why I had pulled over. Then an old lady walked up to the car (with a strong Jamaican accent) and said, *Lady, do you know which way is Pasadena Elementary School?* I responded, *Are you going to vote?* She said, *Yes, my daughter was going to take me when she got off work, but she had to work late, so I am trying to get there before 7:00.* It was about 6:50p.m. I said, *You are not going to make it. Get in and I will take you.* She got in and said, *Oh, thank you. I prayed and asked the Lord to help me get there on time and He sent you. You are my guardian angel!* I gave her my number and told her to call me when she was finished so I could take her back home. When we dropped her off, I looked at my son and said, *Son, that's why we pulled over.* He said, *but you didn't know that lady and you didn't even see her until she came to the car.* I said, *God knows her and sent us to answer her prayer.* That was a divine appointment. Open your eyes to "recognize" divine appointments when you encounter them.

Recognition of Distractions

It is the tactic of Satan to get the children of God off course. If he can divert your mind and attention towards futility, then his tactic is successful. God wants us focused and Christ-centered at all times. People will call you with foolishness and try to get you caught up in their vain endeavors. Keep your mind and your focus prioritized. God is always first, family second, and your highest goals should be thirdly fixated in your mind. Having spiritual insight is the ability to be able to identify distractions. Gossip serves as a distraction. Intermingling in the business of others is a distraction. Focusing upon things that yield no positive fruit serves as a distraction. Even watching vain television shows can be a distraction. Recognize what distracts you and refocus yourself accordingly.

    The bottom line is that achieving prosperity requires both mental and physical exertion. Anything worth having is worth working for and then waiting for. After exerting the time and energy towards the attainment of your goals and putting in the mental strength and necessary actions, you will find that all of your efforts turned out to be far less than the reward received. The time, sacrifice, mental strength and appropriate actions were all seeds sown. But harvest time multiplied the seeds and the blessing is great! You must always keep in mind that prosperity is a mindset and does not necessarily mean money. Money is most times a sign of prosperity, but does not always mean prosperity. It is additionally important not to assume that if people do not have money, they are not blessed. Some of the most blessed people on earth have very little material possessions and they are content with their lives and are at peace. Their souls are rich and that is all that matters to them and to God. Remember this:

> There is wealth under the blessing of God.
> There is wealth under the curse of God.
> There is poverty under the blessing of God.
> There is poverty under the curse of God.

The Cost of the Anointing

There is a powerful prayer in the book of 1 Chronicles 4:10 that is considered a prayer for prosperity. This prayer has proven to bless the lives of many when used over time. When prayed for 30 consecutive days, miraculous things have happened in people's lives. It was a prayer prayed by Jabez, a man whose name defined him to despair and gloom, but he refused to accept the meaning of his name to define His life. He went to the only One who could change the outcome of his life regardless of his name, and that was and still is, the God of Israel, the Eternal God, the heavenly Father and Prince of Peace. The simple prayer is filled with power and when prayed in humility, produces miracles in one's life. The prayer is simply:

...oh Lord, that thou would bless me indeed, and enlarge my territory, that your hand would be with me, and that you would keep me from evil, that I may not cause pain (1 Chronicles 4:10).

In your prayer for the prosperity anointing, also pray for a prosperity consciousness, a vision for spiritual insight, a mind to attract money-begetting ideas, and the wisdom to implement those ideas. I desire to have prosperity in my soul as well as in my life on earth. In my prayer for success and prosperity I ask the Lord to make me a philanthropist and an answered prayer. When people get on their knees with their supplications, I want the Lord to use me to answer their prayers. I want to be an answered prayer! If I can bless a worthy organization with millions of dollars and still have millions more, then what does that say about my bank account? If I can stop someone's home from going into foreclosure then I have served as an answered prayer for them. My heart's desire when it comes to prosperity is to always be a lender, not a borrower, to be above and not beneath, to be the head and not the tail. Therefore, in my claim for prosperity, I say the following out loud as much as I remember to say them:

> I AM a lender, not a borrower.
> I AM above and not beneath.
> I AM the head and not the tail.
> I AM prosperous beyond measure!
> I AM a philanthropist.

If God has given others the prosperity consciousness, He can certainly do the same for you!

CHAPTER ENDING WISDOM KEYS

- Prosperity is a mindset and begins in the mind. Once the mind has been saturated in the understanding of the laws of prosperity, the embodiment of that revelation is manifested in the outward life.

- God is not going to entrust you with thousands of dollars if you have not been faithful with hundreds and He definitely will not entrust you with millions if you have not been faithful with thousands.

- The wealthy have certain patterns of thinking that draws money to them. Their minds are a magnet for money because they have the money consciousness. If people in your town, your city, your state, and your country can become rich, then so can you.

- At different seasons, the tide of opportunity sets in different directions according to the needs of the whole. When the tides advance, there is prosperity; when they recede, there is a recession.

- Both John the Baptist and Judas Iscariot had the same mentor, Jesus. One recognized Him as the Christ, but the other did not and betrayed Him.

Chapter 6
Amazing Grace

For by grace are ye saved through faith; and not of yourselves: it is the gift of God, not of works, lest any man should boast.
(Ephesians 2:8-10).

The Lord of light and glory has poured out His grace upon us through the anointing power of the Holy Ghost. Grace is a priceless gift from God. It is the Father's love towards us, even though we do not deserve it. Amazing grace was bestowed upon us after the ascension of Christ into the Heavenly Sanctuary. When the Savior yielded up His life and with His expiring breath cried out, *"It is finished,"* then the fulfillment of the plan of redemption was assured. The Kingdom of grace was then established. The grace of God in Christ is the foundation of the Christian's hope. As I look back over my life, my heart overflows with gratitude for God's grace that has been poured upon me. My thoughts, deeds, actions and conversations of the past earned me death and eternal damnation, but through grace, repentance and belief in Christ, God has made me joint heirs with Him and has given me an inheritance. Many Christians do not understand the magnitude of God's amazing grace that has been bestowed upon their lives. Grace is popularly and accurately defined as "unmerited favor". When you "merit" something, you earn it, but when it is "unmerited" you have not earned it. With grace, you did not earn salvation or favor, but are receiving the benefits of it anyway. Through God, grace has been given to everyone, which has been made possible only by Jesus Christ. God gave humanity this amazing grace by sending His son to die on a cross by pouring out His soul as an offering for sin, thus delivering us from eternal damnation.

God's grace is available to everyone, including the unsaved. *"For the grace of God that brings salvation hath appeared to all men" (Titus 2:11).* Christ did the work to make salvation available to all. Jesus died as a sacrifice for man because the fallen race could do nothing to recommend themselves to God or earn His grace. God showed His grace by saving us from sin's punishment. God also shows His grace by giving us strength and guidance each day. It is God's grace that protects us from seen and unseen dangers. His grace gives us strength to handle difficult problems and endure disappointments and frustrations. His grace also brings us out of those trials and tribulations and makes us stronger.

FREE-WILL AND SELF-CHOICE

In life, we often make the mistake of blaming God for consequences that result from our own decisions and choices. When the outcome of our choices ends up damaging and disappointing, we blame God and ask Him why He allowed us to endure that. But we must always keep in mind that God gives us free will and self choice. God never forces the will or the conscience, but He does give warnings first. He never just sits and allows us to make mistakes. When He sees us going in the wrong direction or about to make a major mistake, He speaks to us through intuition, whispers, dreams, visions, people, television, radio, etc. He uses the closest and most convenient avenue to deliver you a message of warning. When you ignore the messages or cast them off as not meant for you, then you are left on your own. Warnings always come before destruction. But God, in His amazing grace, still makes a way of escape. He allows us to go through things, but He brings us out after we finally turn to Him for help and guidance. If only we would have sought Him for help and guidance in the beginning! As we grow in grace, in wisdom, and in the knowledge of God, we come to discover that every triumph, disappointment, promotion, demotion, joy, defeat, happiness sadness, failure and success all contributed to making us the person we are today. Those accumulated experiences have made you the unique person that you are right now. This uniqueness distinguishes you from everyone else because no two people have had the exact same experiences. You are rare and there is value in rarity. Therefore you are valuable! There is a reason that you have the personality that you do, the desires that you do, the heart that you do. You are not like everyone else. You are precious and unique in God's sight, so stop trying to "fit in" or wonder why people do not understand you. It is because they do not understand the uniqueness in you and that is just fine. It is not meant for them to understand. Others will be drawn to you because of your uniqueness. He made you unique for His purpose, so just be yourself. Love everybody. Hate nobody. Befriend somebody. Witness to anybody. Let your light shine in this dark world with a smile and some good deeds. Meekness does not mean weakness. It actually means strength. Being kind does not mean that you are weak. It means that you have peace within yourself and have no problem showing it. You never know what your kindness will do to someone just needing a sign that there is still some goodness in this world.

    Life is a journey and an unfoldment and we are constantly discovering things along life's journey. Solomon said in the book of Ecclesiastes, *"In much wisdom is much grief. He that increases understanding increases sorrow (Ecclesiastes 1:18)."* With much wisdom comes knowledge of both good and bad and this discernment can be disheartening at times. For this reason, we must be careful of what we pray for. Discernment is not always a good thing because you discern the truth about things and people and coming into the knowledge of the truth can hurt. We must keep our hearts guarded.

God's desire for His children is for us to live at our greatest potential through the grace that has been bestowed upon us. In order to do this, we must be purged and taken through the fire for purification. After having been exposed to the world for a time, clinging to carnal inclinations, loving the pleasures of the world, allowing our thoughts to feed off of evil impressions, indulging in debauchery and narcissism, engaging in dishonest practices and ignoring the promptings and leading of the Holy Ghost, we must be purged. God allows you to go your own way for a while, but the hour will come when it is time to walk into your destiny. Every believer who desires to walk into the fullness of their calling must have a wilderness experience. In chapter two, when discussing the 'fullness of time', we looked at how Jesus was sent *by the Spirit* into the wilderness to be tempted. *And Jesus being full of the Holy Ghost returned from Jordan and was **led by the spirit** into the wilderness (Luke 4:1)*. It is important to note that not all wilderness experiences are of the devil. In this passage of scripture, Jesus was sent "by the Spirit" into the wilderness. When your season comes, the Spirit will take you into the wilderness for teaching and purging. It is also important to take note that Jesus' wilderness experience came directly after a marvelous event had just transpired in His life. John had just baptized Him in the Jordan River and the Spirit of God descended upon Him in the form of a dove and God's audible voice spoke and said, *This is my beloved son in whom I am well-pleased (Mathew 3:17)*. Jesus had just been given heavenly approval. God had just authenticated Him to go and teach and preach. But directly after that, all hell broke loose. He was sent immediately to the wilderness to be tempted of the devil and He overcame each temptation. We learn from this. After you have experienced a major accomplishment or are acknowledged or praised for a major achievement, be vigilant and clothe yourself in humility because this is the time that Satan will come to knock you off course. He wants to steal that joy.

EMOTIONAL BAGGAGE

We all have some emotional baggage which has resulted because of the things we have gone through in life. Baggage is referred to as leftover feelings resulting from emotional pain and psychological bruising from the past. Baggage usually causes bitterness, fear, doubt, suspicion, distrust, withdrawal, hesitation, or failure to love or be loved; and these feelings are hidden behind a big invisible wall that people walk around with to protect themselves from getting hurt again. When we hear the term 'emotional baggage' we automatically think of women, but men carry emotional baggage inside as well. When this baggage has not been appropriately dealt with, it seeps out little by little and sabotages new relationships that would otherwise have long-term potential.

In order to walk in liberty, live in harmony with others and exude the peace and joy of the Lord, we must get free. Your painful past must be dealt with head on and released. This is called deliverance. Only you know if you still have baggage that causes frustration in your life. If things in your past cause emotions of shame, guilt, anger, bitterness or resentment to rise up inside you when you think about them, then you are not totally delivered. Deliverance means that the memories of those painful events no longer haunt you or cause you to feel bad. You are not less of a person because of those experiences; if anything, consider yourself privileged that God chose you because He knew that you would endure and overcome them.

To hide the baggage of the past, many people mask it by attaching themselves to things and people. Too many people look for happiness and joy outside of themselves, but external conditions and people can never fill a void that you may have. Nothing outside of you can make you happy. We attach ourselves to pleasure because we expect happiness from them forgetting that happiness is found within us. When we expect joy from outside things, we become attached to those things. People think that money will make them happy, but money does not bring happiness. It brings a degree of peace and comfort, but it does not make you happy. Everything you need is found within the reservoir of your soul. Seeking happiness from external things is similar to the story of the Musk Deer. There is an old ancient fable about this animal. It has a scented spot above its forehead that gives off a fragrance. This deer runs here and there, to and fro in search of the scent, not realizing that the scent comes from its own forehead. The deer has been known to even jump off cliffs in search of the scent. It is the same with us as humans. We run after external things thinking they will make us happy (money, possessions, houses and cars) when we already have happiness if we would just take the time to go within. Happiness is found within us.

THE POWER WITHIN

The kingdom of heaven is within you. The Spirit of God is within you. You only have one life and it is up to you to choose to live your life with joy, peace, happiness and harmony or you can choose to live your life with hurt, anger, unforgiveness, and bitterness from things that have happened to you in your past. Bad things happen to good people, but the way you choose to handle the bad things will determine the quality of the lessons learned and the blessings that you will receive from enduring such things. The severity of your test is a good indicator as to the size of the blessing that will manifest afterwards. No matter what happens to you, you must persevere. God has given you inner strength and fortitude to overcome anything that you encounter.

The story of your life on earth has already been written from beginning to end. You may not know what that ending is, but God knows and He will always guide and direct you towards the right path; but once you see the path, you must walk it. There is nothing that can or will happen to you along this journey of life that God has not permitted, but He has already equipped you with unlimited power, supernatural strength and unmitigated gall to conquer everything that comes your way. Power is within you. The kingdom of heaven is within you, therefore the power to overcome any obstacle, challenge, or adversity is within you as well. The story of your life includes the trials, tribulations, hardships, difficulties, victories and triumphs. In order to be victorious, it is necessary for you to go through the hills and valleys, mountaintop experiences, wilderness experiences and also the Calvary and Golgotha experiences. You can and will triumph over any bad situation if you recognize and use the power within, which can only be found through seeking God.

It is written in the book of Jeremiah Chapter 1:5, *before I formed you in the belly, I knew you and before you came forth out of the womb, I sanctified you and ordained you...* The world starts your life with a birth certificate and ends your life with a death certificate, but if God says that He *...knew you "before" you were in the womb,* then you had an existence before you came on earth and you will continue to have an existence after you leave earth. Your spirit is what is eternal. Your flesh is carnal. This means that you are spirit. You already know that God is a spirit. For this reason, we worship Him in spirit and in truth. It is your spirit that worships His Spirit. He breathed His spiritual substance into you and you became a living, breathing, spiritual soul. Therefore, the essence of who you are is spiritual. Your body is not who you *really* are. Your body is only a coat of skin made of dust to contain your spirit until it is time for your spirit to fly away - out of that coat of flesh. Since you are spiritual, you must seek spiritual answers for your problems. The Spiritual is superior to the natural. Natural things are temporary. Spiritual things are eternal. The answers to all of life's problems are found in the Spirit and are also outlined in the Bible through the inspired, Word of God. The spiritual world is invisible to the natural eye and is quiet and unseen, but very powerful and always operating. The most powerful forces in the universe are invisible. Your most powerful forces are invisible as well, but you can tap into your forces through silent meditation and communion with the spiritual part of your being.

UNFORGIVENESS

We cannot talk about grace without talking about forgiveness because grace is given because of forgiveness. The Father has forgiven us through Christ Jesus and we now have access directly into the throne room, the holy of holies because of the veil that has been ripped that once separated us from God. How then can we not forgive others when God has forgiven us? Unforgiveness is the greatest block to healing. Without forgiving, total healing is impossible. Forgiveness is the foundation upon which healing emerges. The inability to forgive has been the most widespread sin that blocks a deliverance from occurring. Unforgiveness is one of the primary tools that Satan uses to gain a stronghold into a believer's life. It is a stronghold, having a very "strong" "hold" on a person. Unforgiveness is one of the most prolific causes of disease. It is a very powerful emotion. Spiritually, it keeps a person in bondage. One is never truly free, nor can they walk in total liberty so long as they are harboring unforgiveness in their heart towards anyone. Unforgiveness is one of Satan's most powerful tools to keep believers in bondage. But you not forgiving someone does not hurt the other person, it only hurts you! After a while, the person who hurt you will forgive themselves and they will move on while you are still harboring on to what they did to you. Forgiveness does not have to mean reconciliation, it means release. It can be one-sided. You do not need the other person in order to forgive them. You simply release what they did from your consciousness. When you think about what they did and it no longer has a painful effect on you, then you know you have released it. Forgiveness is simply a decision made to let it go. It is as easy as that. Forgiveness is not as hard as the devil makes it seem. Unforgiveness is one of the heaviest weights in your emotional baggage bag. When you finally get rid of it, you feel the weight of a heavy burden being lifted. You are a happier and healthier person. It feels so good to live in peace with others and go forward in the joy and freedom of the Lord. Forgiveness brings restoration, healing, and peace.

HUMILITY

Humility comes before exaltation. *Humble yourselves under the mighty Hand of God, that He may exalt you in due time (1 Peter 5:6).* As we study the Word of God with an earnest desire for truth, we begin to learn the patterns of God. We see what moves His heart, what He responds to and how He responds to certain situations and people. Since God is the same yesterday, today and forever, then we know that He does not change. Therefore as we learn how He operates, we can adjust ourselves in heart to be able to get His attention. One thing that stands out to me in the sacred scriptures is how God responds to humility. I have discovered that even after we have sinned, if we humble ourselves in heart, God, in His amazing grace will extend His mercy to us. God has established His law of cause and effect, which cannot be broken, so there is an effect for every cause, but God will show mercy while we are experiencing the consequences of the seeds we have sown. We must resolutely humble ourselves before the Lord and press our petitions at the mercy seat.

Two distinct examples stand out to me where God's heart was touched as a result of humility. The first story is found in the book of 2 Kings 20:1-6. It is the story of Hezekiah, King of Judah who did that which was right in the sight of the Lord. The Bible says that, *"He trusted in the Lord God of Israel; so that after him was none like him among all the kings of Judah, nor any that were before him. He clave to the Lord and departed not from following Him, but kept His commandments, which the Lord commanded Moses. And the Lord was with him and he prospered wherever he went."* But Hezekiah became sick and was about to die. The prophet Isaiah came to Hezekiah with a Word from God telling him to get his house in order because he was going to die. But Hezekiah turned his face to the wall and prayed and cried. He brought God in remembrance of how faithful he had been to Him and how he had walked before Him in truth with a perfect heart. He cried hard before the Lord. He touched the Lord's heart so much that God sent Isaiah the prophet back to Hezekiah with another Word. The Lord said, *Tell Hezekiah that I have heard his prayer, I have seen his tears: behold I will heal him on the third day: ...I will add unto his days fifteen years."* God hears the prayers of the heart. That story touched me on many levels and helped me to see that God is a God of mercy.

The next story is that of a wicked King named Ahab. It is written that, *Ahab did evil in the sight of the Lord above all that were before him (1 Kings 16:30).* The Word also says, *"as if it had been a light thing for him to walk in the sins of Jeroboam...*

he took to wife Jezebel the daughter of Ethbaal king of the Zidonians, and went and served Baal (a false God) and worshipped him. Not only was this king wicked and evil above all who were before him, but he made matters worse by marrying a wicked and controlling false prophetess named Jezebel. In 1 Kings 21:25-26, it reads, *But there was none like unto Ahab, which did sell himself to work wickedness in the sight of the Lord, whom Jezebel his wife stirred up. And he did very abominably in following idols, according to all things as did the Amorites, whom the Lord cast out before the children of Israel.* After having done so much evil and even allowing his wife to influence him into more evil, God's judgment was finally passed upon Ahab through the prophet Elijah: *Thou has sold thyself to work evil in the sight of the Lord. Behold, I will bring evil upon thee, and will take away thy posterity, and will cut off from Ahab him that pisseth against the wall, and him that is shut up and left in Israel, and will make thine house like the house of Jeroboam...says the Lord (1 Kings 21:21-22).* Ahab was no doubt a wicked king. But look at what happens next: 27: *and it came to pass that when Ahab heard those words, that he rent his clothes, and put sackcloth upon his flesh, and fasted, and lay in sackcloth, and went softly. And the word of the Lord came to Elijah the Tishbite saying,* 29: *Seest thou how Ahab* **humbled** *himself before me? Because he* **humbled** *himself before me, I will not bring the evil in his days: but in his son's days will I bring the evil upon his house.* God did not take the judgment away, but in His mercy and grace, He postponed it. Even though Ahab was one of the most evil kings in the history of the Israelites, God's heart was still touched through Ahab's humility and because of his humility, God extended His mercy. How much more mercy and amazing grace will He extend to His own children when we humble ourselves before Him? Humility touches the heart of God.

PRAISE & WORSHIP

Amazing grace allows us into the inner court, which is the holy of holies. Through prayer, praise and worship, we access God. There is no longer a veil that separates us from God. We have direct access to Him now. In the book of Psalms, it is written that everything that has breath must praise the Lord. To praise God is to show gratitude for what He has done for us. When we praise Him, we thank Him for His grace and mercy. We lift Him up because of His goodness. When we praise Him, we may sing, dance, play musical instruments and rejoice in Him because of His great love. However, worship is distinctly different from praise. Worship requires self-discipline. It is more solemn, more attentive and contemplative. It is sometimes silent; little is spoken but the thankful heart and tears. Worship is not about how loud you can become, but how quiet can you be in His Presence. We pray as humans, but we worship as angels! Anyone can praise God. Anyone can enter the service and join in the praise songs, dance the dance and play the musical instruments, but those who have relationship, are those who worship. Praise is standing up, but worship is bowing down. Those who know what it is like to experience the fire and come out of it, worship Him. Those who have been through the wilderness experience and have come out of it, worship Him. Those who have been forgiven much, love much and they worship Him. Worshipping Him is to enter His gates with thanksgiving and into His courts with Praise. Worship is meditative. When you have been elevated in the spirit realm, you worship Him. Worship is intimate.

JACOB'S LADDER

In the book of Genesis 28:12, Jacob had a dream, and in the dream he saw a vision of a ladder which was between heaven and earth. God's angels were ascending and descending on the ladder and God was standing above the ladder. *And he dreamed, and behold a ladder set up on the earth, and the top of it reached to heaven: and behold the angels of God ascending and descending on it (Genesis 28:12).* Those angels represent the messengers that go to and from the earth. The angels that are ascending (going up) are going back to heaven from the earth taking the prayers of the righteous up to God. The ones that are descending (going down) are going to the earth to deliver the answered prayers to the people of God. The trip is not always a direct route. Angels are constantly derailed by evil forces in the atmosphere. They are constantly fighting with principalities, powers, and rulers of the darkness of this world. Satan is constantly trying to prevent prayers from God's children from reaching the throne room, but fights even harder to prevent the blessings or answered prayers from reaching the people of God on earth.

    There are things that we can do as believers in Christ to expedite our answered prayers and blessings. Faith without works is dead. We must put in some work! We can enter warfare with the war angels and come against those forces that have come against us. Angels are fighting for us in the spirit realm and we can fight for ourselves from the earth realm, but enter the spirit realm through prayer. We must use the weapon of our tongue to bind and loose. We must speak directly to those forces and take authority over them in the name of Jesus using the blood of Jesus! Speak these proclamations and decrees out of your mouth confidently, with conviction and resolutely. Speak directly into your circumstances and command it to turn around for your good. If the enemy has stolen from you, take authority over the enemy using the weapons of your warfare and command them to loose everything that has been stolen and to restore seven fold what was taken. You can do it. You have the power within you to come against these forces. The people of God just don't use the power they have. It's time to rise up in this season and enter spiritual warfare for what is rightfully yours!

THE POWER OF PRAYER

From the secret places of prayer come powers that shake the world. Your prayer life should be a continuous, daily and automatic practice. Prayer should be as automatic as brushing your teeth. At the very minimum, people brush once a day, but some brush two and three times a day. The number of times that you brush your teeth should never exceed the amount of times that you pray. A tactic of Satan is to make the people of God think that their prayers are not being heard. He heaps the burdens upon us at times so that we will believe that our prayers are going no farther than the ceiling, but understand that when things "seem" to be getting worse, that's because the blessing is on the way and the enemy of your faith wants you to doubt the promises of God so that eventually you will speak a word of doubt so strongly that you will abort the blessing that was just about to manifest. That's how powerful your spoken words are. In the book of Daniel, chapter 10, we see what happens sometimes when we pray. Sometimes our prayers are held up. When our prayers are released from the earth, they must go through three layers in order to reach God: the outer court, the inner court, and finally the holy of holies, which is the third heaven. The job of the devil is to intercept those prayers. There are evil forces and principalities that we must contend with in the invisible world. Their job is to stop the answered prayers from reaching the earth and to keep the people of God in bondage, oppression and frustration.

Satan's policy is to block our prayers from entering the throne room where God is. *Then said he unto me, fear not, Daniel: for from the first day that you did set your heart to understand and to chasten yourself before your God, your words were heard, and I have come for your words. But the prince of the kingdom of Persia withstood me one and twenty days: but, lo, Michael, one of the chief princes, came to help me; ...Now I am come to make thee understand what shall befall thy people in the latter days: for yet the vision is for many days (Daniel 10:12-14).* Note what the angel said: "from the first day that you set your heart to understand and to chasten yourself before your God, your words were heard." The angel was dispatched to Daniel the day that he prayed and was sent immediately to bring the answer, but was "held up" by a demonic power until Michael the war angel came to assist him and free him up so that he could deliver the Word from the Lord. It is sometimes like that when we pray. We wonder why our prayers are not answered right away and why we have to pray the same prayer for weeks, months and even years. Maybe God answered your prayer the first time you prayed it, but it is "held up." Perhaps you need to join that spiritual battle by using the power of your tongue to bind and loose, uproot, thrown down, build and plant. You can enter spiritual warfare on your own behalf, understanding that you are not fighting with natural beings. *For we wrestle not against flesh and blood, but against principalities, against powers, against the rulers of the darkness of this world, against spiritual wickedness in high places (Ephesians 6:12).* Know the power that you have in God and begin using that power.

    Spiritual warfare is serious. It is a real war that you enter and takes strong soldiers to fight. Entering spiritual warfare takes boldness, courage, confidence and assurance of who you are in Christ. You must be equipped with the armor of God on and you must already be known in the spirit realm. If you do not have a constant and consistent prayer life; if you have a shaky relationship with the Lord and weak study of the scriptures, then do not try to enter spiritual warfare. You must build yourself up in the most holy faith first. If you do try to enter spiritual warfare with a shaky foundation, you may become like the seven sons of Sceva in Acts 19:11-16:

> *And God wrought special miracles by the hands of Paul.*
>
> *So that from his body were brought unto the sick handkerchiefs or aprons, and the diseases departed from them, and the evil spirits went out of them.*
>
> *Then certain of the vagabond Jews, exorcists, took upon them to call over them which had evil spirits the name of the Lord Jesus, saying, "We adjure you by Jesus whom Paul preacheth."*
>
> *And there were **seven sons of one Sceva**, a Jew, and chief of the priests, which did so.*
>
> ***And the evil spirit answered and said, Jesus I know, and Paul I know, but who are ye?***
>
> *And the man in whom the evil spirit was **leaped on them, and overcame them, and prevailed against them**, so that they fled out of that house naked and wounded.*

The spirits in the above scripture flat out said, *Jesus I know and Paul I know, but WHO ARE YOU?* If you have not been in the spirit realm long enough, DO NOT enter spiritual warfare! You are not known and you will get defeated. Gird up your loins and become known in the spirit realm. It is fine if you are not ready for warfare right now as long as you are seeking to become stronger in the Lord. You must crawl before you walk and walk before your run. You start with a constant and consistent prayer life and a consistent reading of the Word. Consistency is the key. God will strengthen your spirit man when you show yourself worthy through consistency and faithfulness in prayer and study. You can do all things through Christ who strengthens you!

CHAPTER ENDING WISDOM KEYS

- As we grow in grace, in wisdom, and in the knowledge of God, we come to discover that every triumph, disappointment, promotion, demotion, joy, defeat, happiness, sadness, failure and success all contributed to making us the person we are today.

- God allows you to go your own way for a while, but the hour will come when it is time to walk into your destiny. Every believer who desires to walk in the fullness of their calling must have a wilderness experience.

- The inability to forgive has been the most widespread sin that blocks a deliverance from occurring. Unforgiveness is one of the primary tools that Satan uses to gain a stronghold into a believer's life.

- From the secret places of prayer come powers that shake the world!

- Spiritual warfare is serious. It is a real war that you enter into and takes strong soldiers to fight. Entering spiritual warfare takes boldness, courage, confidence and assurance of who you are in Christ. You must be equipped with the armor of God on and you must already be known in the spirit realm.

Chapter 7
Holding on to His Promises

> *So shall my Word be that goeth forth out of my mouth: it shall not return unto me void, but it shall accomplish that which I please, and it shall prosper in the thing whereto I sent it.*   *(Isaiah 55:11-12)*

The promises of God and *yea* and *Amen*. As we consider our individual lives, the ups and downs, victories and defeats, happiness and sadness, we may wonder what this whole experience on earth is all about. What is it all for? It is because God has called each of us to contribute to His eternal plan for salvation. We each have a vital part to play in God's overall plan. You are not an accident or a mistake. I do not care if your mother tried to abort you, a sickness tried to kill you or the doctor said that you would not live past a certain timeframe, the fact that you are still here is because you were a part of God's eternal plan. The assignment that each of us has been given cannot be carried out by anyone other than us. Most people do not know who they are and far more are confused about their assignment here on this earth. God knows everything. He already knows the outcome of your life from the beginning to the end. Anytime God (through His prophets) asks a question, it is never so He can get clarity. He only asks so that YOU can get clarity. He wants you to gain a greater revelation about yourself. When God asked Adam, *"Where are you,"* it was not because He didn't know where Adam was, but because Adam himself did not know where He was anymore in relation to God. When God asked him, *"Where are you?"* God was not talking about a place or space, He was talking about identity. God knew where Adam was both in the natural and in the Spirit, but He needed Adam to recognize this. God will not strive with man forever. He is slowly withdrawing His Spirit from the earth. As men and women continue to reject the teachings of His Word, God withdraws His Spirit and leaves the lovers of falsehood to the deceptions which they cling to. When iniquity is full, the despisers of God will learn too late that it is a fearful thing to have worn out divine patience. The restraining Spirit of God, which imposes a check upon the cruel power of Satan will be removed. But Christ continues to intercede on our behalf and light will be given to those who seek it. Do you know where you are (in God)?

Our entire journey on earth contributes to God's plan in some mysterious way and if we stay close to Him, connected to His Holy Spirit and consumed in the study of His Word, we will be able to clearly see our role in His eternal plan and govern our lives accordingly. The end result of it all is Christ. Everything is summed up in Christ Jesus.

THE SACRED SCRIPTURES

The Word of God is the greatest and most precious treasure in both heaven and earth. It reveals all the promises of God and opens up the plan of salvation. The Bible is a valuable roadmap for the children of God. We must eat the whole Word. It amazes me when discussing the Word of God in Sunday School or in friendly Christian conversations that someone will say, *"...but that's the old testament"* when a scripture is quoted from it. I never could and still do not understand what that statement means and I have heard it said many times. Are they implying that we are to cast aside what is written in the Old Testament and focus only on the New Testament for life application? God has not abolished any part of the Bible. Every inspired Word in both the Old and New Testament is relevant, pertinent and applicable to the present day.

The Word of God is a record of God's dealings with men in the past, a revelation of the duties and responsibilities of the present, and an unfoldment of the glories and perils of the future. His Word is a revelation of Himself. Every new truth discerned is a fresh disclosure of the character of God. Both witnesses, the Old and the New Testament point to the plan of salvation. The types, sacrifices and prophecies of the Old Testament point to the Savior to come. The gospels and epistles of the New Testament tell of a Savior who has already come in the exact manner foretold by prophecy. As you study the Word of God with a pure heart and desire for the truth, angels of heaven will be by your side and rays of light will shine from heaven and reveal the treasures of truth to your understanding.

There is a strong power in the Holy Scriptures that strengthens the believer in mind, body and spirit. The Word of God is to be studied with an open heart through the power of the Holy Spirit. The Holy Spirit of God must be present when studying. When the Bible is studied from human wisdom and human intellect only, intellectual comprehension of doctrine is obtained, but the Spirit is void. When studying the Word of God, human reasoning is to be cast aside and the Spirit of God is to do the teaching. By faith through the Spirit are we to receive Godly wisdom contained in the Holy Scriptures. The plan of salvation is clearly revealed in the sacred pages and we should find comfort, hope, and peace in believing in Jesus from both the Old and New Testament. Many believers often refer to the Old Testament as 'The Law' and the New Testament as 'Grace', but if we read the New Testament with an old covenant heart, it will just be law to us. If we read the Old Testament with only a new covenant heart, we will cast aside God's commandments which are needful for us in this present day. The old covenant is the letter; the new covenant is the Spirit. We need both the letter and the Spirit in order to bring us into the completeness of the revelation of Christ. The Old Testament points us to the Gospel and the Gospel leads us to a more exact fulfilling of the law. They go hand-in-hand. The righteousness of the law is fulfilled in us, through grace and faith which is in Christ Jesus. By the law is the knowledge of sin; and not until we are convicted of sin will we truly feel the need for the atoning blood of Christ. There is no evidence in the scriptures that the Ten Commandments or any part of the Old Testament has been abolished or changed. Of course, the customs and practices of those times have changed to meet the demands of the present age. The information of those times is given to us in the scriptures so that we will know what their customs and practices were and gain a better understanding of those times, but the commandments and principles of God have not changed and never will change. What God has established, no man can overthrow. Not one Word of God will return back to Him void. The Law of God is a revelation of His will, a transcript of His character and will forever endure as a faithful witness in heaven. Not one commandment has been annulled, not a jot or tittle has been altered. All of God's commandments are sure. They stand fast forever. Every part of God's law must remain in force upon all mankind and in all ages. Jesus said, *I am not come to destroy the law, but to fulfill it.* Let's accept the Holy Scriptures, all of it, with implicit faith.

The Bible is the only supreme, infallible authority. As children of God, it is of vital importance to our soul that we make designated time to study God's Word. The study of the scriptures is the means divinely ordained to bring the children of God into closer connection with their Creator and to give them a clearer knowledge of His will. Many do not know the will of God for their lives because they do not take the time to spend with Him through prayer and/or the study of His Word. Prayer and study go hand-in-hand. Having a consistent prayer life is wonderful, but you must also have consistent time for study of the Bible. One without the other is incomplete. We must not rely upon the preacher or the television evangelist to give us our knowledge of what is written in the Word. They make mistakes sometimes. The precepts of scripture conveyed through the understanding are to rule your conscience. In other words, God speaking to you through your study of the Bible is the one infallible guide. You must know the Word of God for yourself! *Study to show thyself approved unto God, a workman that needs not to be ashamed, rightly dividing the word of truth (2 Timothy 2:15-16).* Devote yourself with your whole soul to the search after divine truth. Invoke the aid of the Holy Spirit. The Word of God is plain in itself. If there appears any obscurity in one place, the Holy Ghost, who is never contrary to Himself explains the same more clearly in other places. When God's children neglect to search the scriptures for themselves, they are led to accept false interpretations and cherish doctrines which have no foundation in the Bible.

    Not only does study of the Word open up treasures of truth, but if studied with an open heart for the truth through the Spirit, it will change the very personality of the believer. When you are engrossed in earnest reading of the Word, something begins to happen in you. The Word begins to change your DNA and you will find that you are no longer the person you once were. When the Word gets on the inside of you, it becomes an applied Word and presses out of you and you begin living it. The scriptures give transforming, educating, power that expands the mind, sharpens the perceptions and ripens the judgment. It gives stability of purpose, patience, courage and fortitude; it refines your character and sanctifies your soul. Between your private, personal prayer time with the Lord and your study of His Word, a new Creation emerges. When you stand on the Word of God, your faith increases and nothing can shake that faith because you are rooted and grounded in Christ. Your hands are laid confidently into the Hands of Christ and your feet are planted upon the Rock of Ages.

BRING HIM IN REMEMBRANCE

It moves the heart of God when we bring Him in remembrance of His Word. The Word of God must become part of you. It must get all in your spirit and become part of who you are. You will not always have the Bible around. There will be situations where you will have to use the sword of the Spirit, which is the Word of God and there will be no Bible to pick up and search for scriptures. For this reason, you must memorize powerful scriptures. You may need God to get you out of trouble and praying to Him is fine, in fact it is crucial, but when you pray His Word back to Him, that gets His attention! Learn to give God His Word back to Him. He encourages us to do that. In fact, in Isaiah 43:26, He says, *Put me in remembrance.* Bring back to God what He has said about you. Heaven and earth will pass away, but the Word of God will never pass away. His Word shall not return back to Him void. If He spoke it, it HAS to come to pass, so remind Him of what He said about you. Do not doubt what God has said in His Word. If you doubt what is written in His word, then you have no hope, nothing to look forward to; you have nothing! The Word of God is true from beginning to end. It will come to pass if God spoke it. Even if the promise has been delayed, it will not be denied. God said in Jeremiah 1:12, *I hasten my Word to perform it.* To hasten means to hurry, so remind Him of that! Is there anything above the name of Jesus? Think about this question for a moment. Yes, there is one thing above the name of Jesus and that is HIS WORD. He says in Psalm 138:2, *thou has magnified thy Word above all thy name.* His Word is so important to Him that He has placed it higher than His own name. So what has He said about you? Bring Him in remembrance of His Word!

LIGHT & DARKNESS

In the beginning was the Word, and the Word was with God, and the Word was God (John 1:1). You cannot separate God from His Word because God *is* His Word, so as you study the Word of God, you are actually spending time with Him because He is His Word. *In Him was life; and the life was the light of men. And the light shines in darkness; and the darkness comprehended it not (John 1:4).* The scripture above says that the light shines in the darkness. Light and darkness cannot dwell together because they do not agree. One will dominate. It is your responsibility to ensure that the light of God's Word constitutes your mind, body and soul. In Genesis 1:4, God divided the light from the darkness. When you were born again, God immediately began to separate the light from the darkness in your life. As believers, our goal is to walk in the light as He is in the light. *But if we walk in the light, as He is in the light, we have fellowship one with another, and the blood of Jesus Christ his Son cleanses us from all sin (1 John 1:7-9).* As you begin to read and study the Word of God consistently, it will slowly but surely drive out any darkness there may be in you because the Word of God is light. The more light you get inside you through the Word, the less darkness there will be. Eventually you will radiate all light and will find that you are a whole new person. When you walk in light, you walk in truth. You are in the world, but not of the world. That is the power of the Word of God and what it will do in you and through you. For this reason, Satan tries to keep the people of God out of God's Word. If you have a prayer life, but your study time is lacking, then Satan will take that. If you have study time, but your prayer time is lacking, he will take that, but when you have both a strong prayer life and consistent designated time for study, you are powerful and can shake heaven and hell. The Word of God is the most powerful weapon on earth when used strategically. *It is quick and powerful, and sharper than any two-edged sword, piercing even to the dividing asunder of soul and spirit, and of the joints and marrow, and is a discerner of the thoughts and intents of the heart (Hebrews 4:12).* The written Word of God will measure the character of every man. The Word of God is the only infallible authority and the death of Christ is the only complete sacrifice. An intense study of the Word through the Holy Spirit will lead you to the truths of God. The light of God is the anointing of God.

As we hold on to God's promises, we hide them in our hearts so that we will have the Word of God in us at all times. When Satan comes to cause you to doubt God by looking at things in the natural, begin to quote the Word of God starting with this one: *Casting down imaginations, and every high thing that exalts itself against the knowledge of God, and bringing into captivity every **thought** to the obedience of Christ (I Corinthians 10:5).* If a thought comes to you that does not bear good fruit, is not peaceful, loving or kind, it is not from God. Quoting the above verse will bring into subjection every thought that is contrary to the Word of God. After that, begin quoting OUT LOUD some scriptures that you have memorized. The reason for speaking out loud is because words are things and when released from the mouth into the atmosphere, will go out and bring back the tangible equivalent of what you have spoken. You attract what you speak about. When you use the power of the spoken Word of God, you change your conditions, your state of mind and your reality. The more specific you are when speaking, the quicker the manifestation will be and the more powerful the materialization will be. We decree things in our lives one word at a time and with strong convictions. Strong statements produce strong results. Your words always come back to you - for better or for worse. Use the Word of God as your weapon. Below are some promises in the Word of God that you may begin memorizing if you need a starting place.

- I can do all things through Christ who strengthens me. (Philippians 4:13)

- There is therefore now no condemnation to them who are in Christ Jesus, who walk not after the flesh, but after the Spirit. (Romans 8:1)

- But my God shall supply all my needs according to His riches in glory by Christ Jesus. (Philippians 4:18)

- Trust in the Lord with all your heart, and lean not to your own understanding; In all your ways acknowledge Him, and He shall direct your paths. (Proverbs 3:5)

- I once was young and now am old, yet I have never seen the righteous forsaken nor his seed begging for bread. (Psalm 37:25)

- And we know that all things work together for good to them that love God, to them who are the called according to His purpose. (Romans 8:28)

- For I know the thoughts that I think toward you, says the Lord, thoughts of peace, and not of evil, to give you an expected end. (Jeremiah 29:11)

- They that wait upon the Lord shall renew their strength, they shall mount up with wings as eagles. They shall run and not be weary, and they shall walk, and shall not faint. (Isaiah 40:31)

- Thou wilt keep him in perfect peace, whose mind is stayed on thee: because he trusts in thee. (Isaiah 26:3)

- For our light affliction, which is but for a moment, is working for us a far more exceeding and eternal weight of glory. (2nd Corinthians 4:17)

- Ask, and it shall be given you; seek, and ye shall find; knock, and it shall be opened unto you. (Mathew 7:7)

- Delight thyself also in the Lord; and He shall give you the desires of your heart. (Psalm 37:4)

- But seek ye first the kingdom of God and His righteousness; and all these things shall be added unto you. (Mathew 6:33)

- If thou shall confess with thy mouth the Lord Jesus, and shall believe in thine heart that God hath raised Him from the dead, thou shall be saved. (Romans 10:9)

- If my people, who are called by my name, will humble themselves and pray and seek my face and turn from their wicked ways, then I will hear from heaven and forgive their sins and will heal their land. (2 chronicles 7:14)

- If any man be in Christ, he is a new creature: old things are passed away; behold, all things are become new. (2nd Corinthians 5:17)

These are just a few scriptures to get your started, but the sacred scriptures are filled with God's promises to you. Begin resonating on the Word of God and watch how your entire life changes for the better. Your perspective about things will change and your focus will be less on the natural and more on the spiritual. Remember to bring God in remembrance of His Word. He delights in that!

THE SECRET PLACE

Psalm 91 is one of my favorite Psalms. In the first two verses are written, *He that dwells in the* **secret place** *of the most High shall abide under the shadow of the Almighty. I will say of the Lord, He is my refuge and my fortress: my God; in Him will I trust.* When I look at the first verse, I desire to be in the "secret place" so that I can dwell under the shadow of the Almighty. My secret place is my closet. That is where I pray, worship, praise, and cry out to God. That is where He meets me. Sometimes He is there at the "secret place" before I am. There have been times when I have been in the bed past my normal worship time and I can sense that the Lord is already there waiting for me. When you have a designated time and place to meet the Lord and you are consistent in going, you will find that He will meet you there. You will not have to usher in His presence because He is already there. He delights in your praise and worship and He never inhabits your praises without leaving a blessing behind. You were created to worship. God has given you many other things to enjoy in this life, but your main reason for being here on this earth is to praise and worship your Creator, the One who knew you before you were in the womb. When you MAKE designated time to spend with Him in prayer, praise, and worship, you get His favor, His blessings and His power. Make the time to spend with Him today and every day.

In writing on this subject, a memorable experience comes to mind. It happened on the day that I was being licensed to minister and I was to preach my initial sermon. I had been praying about the message that the Lord would have me to speak to the people of God. Months before that, I had been praying about my spiritual prayer language. To me, my tongues were stale and powerless. I had been speaking the same prayer language for years and I felt that my tongues were not effective anymore. My own son would say, *"Mom, you always say the same thing in tongues."* And he could mimic me exactly. Therefore, I did not use my tongues often. My sermon was to be preached on Sunday at 4:00p.m on this particular day. When I woke up that morning, the Lord spoke to me and said, *"I am waiting for you. I have something to give you."* His Words came to me very clearly. However, it was cold in the house so I told the Lord that I would turn off the AC and then after it cooled down, I would come. After turning the air off, I got back into the bed. Sad to say, I fell back to sleep and didn't wake back up until it was time for church. I did not meet the Lord that morning. I felt that I had missed out on what He had for me. Nonetheless, I still met Him when I came home from church before my sermon was to be

Holding on to His Promises

preached at 4:00. I began praising Him, thanking Him and loving on Him. As my hands were lifted up, I heard Him say, *"Open your mouth."* I opened my mouth and many different spiritual languages began pouring out of me. My mouth was speaking uncontrollably and there was a lot of conversation going on. The tongues were fresh, vibrant, new and powerful. God not only refreshed my prayer language that day, but He also gave me diver's tongues - on the day that I preached my first sermon. That evening after I preached, He told me to begin prophesying to the people, but I was afraid and did not do it. Although I knew there was a big angel standing behind me, I was still afraid. However, God understands our human frailties and has mercy upon us. I learned a few things about God that day.

1. He is not like man. Even though I did not come to Him when He called me initially, He did not take the gift away. He gave it to me when I finally came (Man would have said, "You didn't come when I called you, so now you're not getting it!") Thank God that He is not like man.

2. He hears our prayers and in the right season, He will answer them. (I had been praying about my stale tongues for months, but they came right on time)

What is your secret place? If you know that God will meet you at your secret place, then do you have one?

CHAPTER ENDING WISDOM KEYS

♦ God gave His Word as a revelation of Himself. Every new truth discerned is a fresh disclosure of the character of God. Both witnesses, the old and the New Testament point to the plan of salvation.

- When God's children neglect to search the scriptures for themselves, they are led to accept false interpretations and cherish doctrines which have no foundation in the Bible.

- The scriptures give transforming, educating, power that expands the mind, sharpens the perceptions and ripens the judgment. It gives stability of purpose, patience, courage and fortitude; it refines your character and sanctifies your soul.

- The Word of God is true from beginning to end. It will come to pass if God spoke it. Even if the promise has been delayed, it will not be denied.

- It moves the heart of God when we bring Him in remembrance of His Word.

Chapter 8
Victory in Christ

But thanks be to God, which gives us the victory through our Lord Jesus Christ.
1 Corinthians 15:57

Victory in Christ is growing in grace, in knowledge and in wisdom. It is understanding yourself, getting closer to your Creator through prayer and study and knowing how you are to conduct yourself in this world. Victory means knowing who you are in God and whose you are. Walking in victory means monitoring with vigilance, your thoughts, words, and deeds. Sometimes our own words and behaviors can cause problems for us. We often blame the devil for certain hell that breaks loose in our lives, but there are times when Satan has nothing to do with the problems we experience. He just takes the credit and has no problem doing so. We have blamed others for our adversities, but if we were to pull the knife out of our back, we may just find our own fingerprints on it. To be ill-mannered and rude is to be unlearned and unwise. Bad manners are the outward expression of inward defects. You cannot act one way, then say, "I'm not really like that." What you do and say is who you really are and oftentimes your ill-manners and negative speaking causes warfare to break out in your life.

Wisdom shows us where we went wrong, leads us to fully acknowledge our own mistakes, helps us to correct those mistakes, teaches how to act, tells us what to say and the right time to say things and gives us mental and spiritual balance through a change of heart. When the heart changes, the outward behavior changes. Only God can change the heart. One may change their outward behavior temporarily for various deceitful and self-centered reasons while the heart still remains corrupted, but one cannot have a true change of heart without also having a true change in behavior. There are marked indications that one has come into the knowledge of wisdom and power. Below is a list of some of the power that believers use once coming into the knowledge of who they are in God. When we are enlightened by the power that is available to us, in us, and in the sacred scriptures, we become elevated and authoritative in the spirit.

The Power of the Armor of God
This conflict with Satan is spiritual, therefore no tangible weapons can be effectively employed against him or his demons. When we follow God's instructions faithfully and use the weapons available to us, we will be able to stand against the enemy and will have victory regardless of what strategy Satan uses. While in prison in Rome, Paul wrote the Ephesians a letter telling them that the battle takes place in the invisible spiritual realms. It is imperative that we know where the battle is because Satan wants the Lord's warriors to misdirect their energy by fighting against each other (flesh and blood), rather than recognizing that our enemies are spiritual forces operating through others. For this reason, we must keep ourselves covered in the Armor of God. The precious shed blood of Jesus does cover us, but we must also put on the "Whole Armor of God." While we do not see the armor in the natural, it is real in the spirit world. This Armor is absolutely necessary in order to counteract spiritual attacks. When we clothe ourselves with the armor, we step out fully equipped to quench all the fiery darts shot at us by spiritual enemies. A soldier would not go to war without his armor. We are in a spiritual war, and we must certainly not go out

Victory in Christ

into this cruel and dangerous world without the proper spiritual gear.

It is vital to our spiritual body that we put on the whole Armor of God. Keep yourself covered. Be wise as a serpent, but harmless as a dove. At some point, we must become active in the Army of God. In other words, we must become True soldiers. *Be strong in the Lord and in the power of His might. Put on the whole Armor of God, that you may be able to stand against the wiles of the devil. For we wrestle not against flesh and blood, but against principalities, against powers, against the rulers of the darkness of this world, against spiritual wickedness in high places. Wherefore take unto you the whole armor of God, that you may be able to withstand in the evil day, and having done all to stand. Stand therefore, having your loins girded about with truth, and having on the breastplate of righteousness, and your feet shod with the preparation of the gospel of peace; above all, taking the shield of faith wherewith you will be able to quench all the fiery darts of the wicked. And take the helmet of salvation, and the sword of the Spirit, which is the Word of God; praying always with all prayer and supplication in the Spirit, being watchful with all perseverance and supplication for all the saints... (Ephesians 6:10-18).*

The Power of the Holy Spirit
The Holy Spirit is the Third Person of the Godhead, coequal with the Father and the Son. We receive the indwelling of the Holy Spirit the moment we receive Jesus Christ as our Lord and Savior. Jesus sent us this precious gift as a replacement for His absence. With the presence of the Holy Spirit, we have the Spirit of God with us always. We could not have received the gift of the Holy Spirit until after Jesus' ascension. The Father, the Son, and the Holy Spirit are one in power, but distinct in their functions; just as the sun, the light and the heat are one power source, but are

distinct in their functions. In other words, the sun is likened unto the Father, the light from the sun is likened to Jesus, and the heat that we feel is likened unto the Holy Spirit; they all come from the sun (the Father), but are equal in power, yet distinct in their functions.

The Holy Spirit does the work that Jesus did when He was on earth. Just as Jesus convicted the world of sin, the Holy Spirit convicts the world of sin. He is our Helper, Comforter and Guide. The Holy Spirit takes up permanent residence in the hearts of believers and is the revealer of truth. There are many functions of the Holy Spirit, but the main functions are to guide believers into all truth (John 16:13); testify of Jesus (John 15:26); produce His fruit in our lives (Galatians 5:22); and impart believers with spiritual gifts (1 Corinthians 12).

The Power of Spiritual Gifts

Spiritual gifts significantly assist believers in their Christian walk. The power of Spirit-given gifts aids believers in prayer, in spiritual warfare, in edifying the body of Christ, in refreshing the soul, in confusing the enemy and in building up the kingdom of God. In chapter four of this book, great detail was outlined concerning spiritual gifts and how they work in the life of believers. The term "spiritual gifts" comes from the Greek words *charismata* (gifts) and *pneumatika* (spirits). They are the plural forms of *charisma*, meaning "expression of grace" and *pneumatikon* meaning "expression of Spirit". While there are different kinds of gifts, spiritual gifts are God-given graces meant for works of service to benefit and build up the body of Christ as a whole.

The Power of the Tongue

God has given us the gift of being able to clothe thoughts in the form of words. He has enabled us to communicate with each other through words thus, giving us the power to wound or heal, bless or curse, uplift or tear down. This wonderful power of clothing thoughts in the form of words is what differentiates humans from the rest of the animal kingdom. Therefore, if we wish our outward manifestation to be beautiful and strong, we must see that our words are strategically spoken and put together carefully. Words are thoughts and are an invisible power that will finally objectify in the form they are given.

Words often repeated form patterns in the mind which automatically reproduce themselves. Your entire life can be changed for good just by the words that you speak on a daily basis. Your words can magnetize prosperity, harmony, peace, and good toward you or draw trouble, poverty, discord, frustration and evil toward you. You are always attracting or repelling. You attract what you talk about. When you change your belief system in thought, words, and emotional pattern, you change your whole body, you change your situations and you change your reality. The more specific you are when speaking positive, the quicker the manifestation, the greater you feel, the more powerful the materialization. We decree our realities one word at a time. Definite statements produce definite results. Feeling is essential in order for words to manifest. Emotions play a vital role when it comes to manifestation. Whenever you speak with feeling and conviction, you strengthen the magnet within you by attracting the things, people, situations, and resources that correspond with your words and emotions.

The Power of the Mind

The quality of your thought is the measure of your power. The thoughts you think are magnets. They attract things to you. The thoughts that you entertain determines your mental attitude. If your thoughts are negative, you will exude a negative disposition and the words that you speak will be negative, thus attracting negativity to you. If your thoughts are positive, then your conversation will be of a positive nature, thus attracting good to you. Your mental attitude is like a mirror reflecting your thinking. When your mental attitude is positive, your abilities reach a maximum of effectiveness and good results inevitably follow. Your thoughts which lead to your attitude influence people for or against you and it is people that you need in this world to get you where you want and need to go, so why not use the power of thought to influence people for your interests. Every one of your daily secret thoughts are real things, which are acting on the thoughts of other people. A positive attitude is your lottery ticket that will win for you in every situation!

The Power of Self-Confidence
Those who truly know their Lord are some of the most self-confident people are on earth. They may not have a dime in their pockets, but as long as they know they are in right standing with their Creator, nothing else matters. With self-confidence in knowing your God and having the assurance that He knows you, the appearances of problems in the natural do not shake your faith because you stand upon a solid Rock. Your hope is built on nothing less than Jesus' blood and His righteousness. Having self-confidence in knowing who you are gives you boldness in saying what God has instructed you to say. This is not being arrogant or proud; it is being self-assured and confident. Confidence is necessary if you are to teach, preach, evangelize or minister. You must know that you know your Lord and believe on His name if you are to persuade anyone else to know that they know and believe on His name.

RULES OF ENGAGEMENT

The plan of salvation from beginning to end has already been mapped out. We win in the end! We are triumphant through overcoming. Even before Adam fell, God had a plan for the fall and a plan for his restoration. The marriage supper of the lamb was planned thousands of years ahead of schedule. Knowing the rules of engagement and playing them with strategy and precision is key in overcoming. We must study the life of Christ, the patterns of God, and learn the spiritual laws that are in place for our growth and strength. We must then adjust our lives accordingly. When we do this, we will be in harmony with trinity. Just as there are natural laws that should not be broken, there are also spiritual laws that should not be broken. When broken, there are consequences and those consequences can be detrimental.

The Holy Spirit leads us into all truth. There are many interpretations and translations of scripture meanings in the Bible and if not careful, these differences can become the source of division in the body of Christ, which can serve as a distraction for God's people. One common belief among many Christians today is the belief that once a person is saved, they are always saved and will never lose their salvation. Essentially, what is being taught is that once a person accepts Christ Jesus as their Lord and Savior, confesses with their mouth that God has raised Him from the dead, then they are saved forever right then and there. It does not matter what they do after that, they can *never* lose their salvation, but will enter into eternal life. That was a pill that was always hard for me to swallow. As a result, I never swallowed it, but did more scripture searching.

ONCE SAVED ALWAYS SAVED?

I have commonly heard in the Baptist Churches the phrase, *"Once saved, always saved"* and that statement never set right in my Spirit. I am a searcher of the truth and so I researched the Holy Scriptures concerning this matter. When I believe that I have found truth, I meditate on it, then I teach and preach on it. I have found no place in the Bible that supports that statement. When this topic of conversation would come up, I would quote Ezekiel 33:18-19 as my supporting scripture, *When the righteous turns from his righteousness, and commits iniquity, he shall even die thereby. But if the wicked turn from his wickedness, and do that which is lawful and right, he shall live thereby.* But I would get the response, "...*but that's the Old Testament"* so I found a scripture in the New Testament that further supports my belief that a person can lose their salvation. The bottom line is that a believer's name can be written in the Book, but then be blotted out. *He that overcomes, the same shall be clothed in white raiment; and I will not* **blot out** *his name out of the book of life, but I will confess his name before my Father, and before his angels. Revelation 3:5.* This scripture alone implies that a name that was once written in the Book of Life can be blotted out.

THE SANCTUARY

The term "sanctuary" in the Bible, refers to the tabernacle built by Moses. The command to build a sanctuary for the Lord was given to Moses while in the Mount with God. *Let them make me a sanctuary that I may dwell among them (Exodus 25:8).* God Himself gave Moses the plan for the structure and complete directions were given to him for the construction of it. The sanctuary in heaven, where Jesus now ministers on our behalf is the great original. The sanctuary built by Moses was a copy of what is in heaven. The earthly sanctuary was a figure for the time then present, in which were offered both gifts and sacrifices. This sanctuary had two holy places, the *Holy* (inner court) and the *Holy of Holies*, which were *"patterns of things in the heavens" (Hebrews 9:23).* Upon this altar were consumed all the sacrifices offered to the Lord and consumed by fire from the Lord. God required animal sacrifices in order to provide a temporary covering of sins and to foreshadow the perfect and complete sacrifice of Jesus Christ (Leviticus 4:35; 5:10).

    For the sin offering, the repentant sinner would bring their sacrifice (an animal without spot or blemish) to the door of the tabernacle. They would then place their hand upon the animal's head and confess their sins, thus transferring their own sins to the innocent animal sacrifice. By the sinner's own hand the animal was then slain with a knife. After a sin offering was presented, the blood was carried into the holy place by the priest, sprinkled before the veil and placed upon the horns of the golden altar. The fat was consumed by the Lord upon the altar of burnt offering in the court, but the body of the animal was burned outside of the camp. The sins of the people were transferred (in figure) to the officiating priest, who was a mediator for the people. The priest could not become an offering for sin himself and make atonement with his own life because he too was a sinner. Therefore, instead of suffering death himself, an animal without spot or blemish was killed. The penalty of sin was then transferred to the innocent animal, which became his substitute. This symbolized the perfect offering of Jesus Christ. Through the blood of this victim, man looked forward by faith to the blood of Christ which would atone for the sins of the world. *"Without the shedding of blood there is no forgiveness" (Hebrews 9:22).* By this ritual, a substitute had been accepted in the sinner's stead. By the offering of blood, the sinner acknowledged the authority of the Law, confessed the guilt of their transgression, and expressed their faith in Him who was to take away the sins of the world.

    On the Day of Atonement, the high priest was to take two male goats for a sin offering. One goat was sacrificed as a sin offering for the people of Israel (Leviticus 16:15), while the other goat was released into the wilderness to be the scapegoat

(Leviticus 16:20-22). At the door of the tabernacle, the priest laid his hands upon the head of the scapegoat and confessed over him *"all the iniquities of the children of Israel, and all their transgressions in all their sins, putting them upon the head of the goat."* The sin offering provided forgiveness, while the other goat provided the removal of sin. The high priest, having taken an offering for the congregation, went into the Holy of Holies with the blood from the first goat and sprinkled it upon the mercy seat, above the tables of the Law. The broken laws of God had demanded the lives of the sinners, but were now satisfied. During this time, all Israel were required to gather around the sanctuary, and in the most solemn manner, humble their souls before God so that they would receive the pardon of their sins and not be cut off from the congregation.

Since Satan is the originator of sin and the direct instigator of all sins, justice demands that he suffer the final punishment. Christ's work for the redemption of believers will be closed by the removal of sin and the placing of these sins upon Satan, who will bear the final penalty. As the goat bearing these sins was sent away, they were regarded as forever separated from the people. *The scapegoat, bearing the sins of Israel, was sent away, unto a land not inhabited (Leviticus 16:22).* As the priest, in removing the sins from the sanctuary, confessed them upon the head of the scapegoat, so Christ, our High Priest will place all these sins upon Satan, the originator and instigator of sin. Christ was the foundation and life of the temple. The services that were performed were characteristic of the sacrifice of the Son of God. The priesthood was established to represent the character and work of Christ. The entire plan of sacrificial worship was a foreshadowing of the Savior's death, the Redeemer of the world. Since the whole ritual was symbolical of Christ, it had no value apart from Him. When the Jews sealed their rejection of Christ by delivering Him to death, they rejected all that gave significance to the temple and its services. Its sacredness had departed. From that day, the sacrificial offerings and the services connected with them were meaningless. They were left in total darkness to continue their futile sacrifices and offerings. They had no knowledge of Christ as the true sacrifice and the only mediator between God and man. *...we have a High Priest, who is set on the right Hand of the throne of the Majesty in the heavens; a Minister of the sanctuary, and of the true tabernacle, which the Lord pitched, and not man (Hebrews 8:1-2).* In putting Christ to death, the Jews virtually destroyed their temple. When Christ was crucified, the inner veil of the temple was split in two from top to bottom, signifying that the great and final sacrifice had been made, and that the system of sacrificial offerings was forever at an end. *Behold, the Lamb of God, which taketh away the sins of the world (John 1:29).* The slaying of the Passover Lamb was a shadow of the death of Christ. *Christ our Passover is sacrificed for us (1 Corinthians 5:7).* Here is revealed the sanctuary of the New Covenant.

    The sanctuary of the first covenant was pitched by man, built by Moses. The Heavenly Sanctuary is pitched by the Lord, not by man. In the earthly sanctuary, the priest performed their services. The priests who offered gifts according to the law served *...unto the example and shadow of heavenly things (Hebrews 8:5).* Animal sacrifices have ended because Jesus Christ was the ultimate and complete sacrifice. John the Baptist recognized this when he saw Jesus coming to be baptized and said, "*Behold, the lamb of God who takes away the sin of the world!" (John 1:29).* Animal sacrifices came to an end with Jesus Christ, the precious Lamb that was slain. Jesus Christ was the ultimate and final sacrificial substitute (Hebrews 7:27) and is now the only mediator between God and humanity (1 Timothy 2:5).

THE BOOKS

As Christians, we also hear much conversation about the 'Book of Life' and that our ultimate Christian goal is to have our names written in that book; but the Book of Life is just one of many books kept on record in heaven. *And I saw the dead, small and great, stand before God; and the books were opened: and another book was opened, which is the book of life: and the dead were judged out of those things which were written in the books, according to their works. (Rev. 20:12).* Before you entered this earth, there was a book written and sealed just for you. No one was worthy to loose the seal of your book other than the Lamb of God. The books in heaven, in which the names and the deeds of every person are registered, are to determine the decision of the judgment. Both the living and the dead are to be judged *"out of those things which were written in the books, according to their works."* Sins that have not been repented of will not be pardoned or blotted out of the books of record, but will stand as a witness against the sinner in the Day of Judgment. The sinner may have committed their evil deeds in the light of day or in the darkness of night, but those sins are open and manifest before God. Angels of God witnessed each sin and registered them in the unerring records. Those sins may have been concealed, denied or covered up from father, mother, wife, husband, children, and/or associates and no one but the guilty sinner may cherish any suspicion of the wrong, but it is laid bare and open before the intelligences of heaven. Angels have registered both the good and the evil of every person. The mightiest conqueror, the most powerful leader or the most brilliant genius cannot call back the records of even a single day. Our acts, our words, even our most secret motives, all have their weight in deciding our destiny for eternal life or eternal damnation. Though our past sins may be forgotten by us, they will bear testimony to justify or condemn us if not confessed. The hidden selfishness of men stands revealed in the

Victory in Christ

books of heaven. There is the record of unfulfilled duties to our fellow brothers and sisters in Christ and forgetfulness of our Savior's Words, commandments and ordinances. In judgment, we will see how often we gave Satan the time that belonged to Christ. Sad is the record which angels bear to heaven. Professed followers of Christ are absorbed in acquiring worldly possessions and the enjoyment of earthly pleasures. Money, time and strength are sacrificed for display and self-indulgence; but few are the moments devoted to God in prayer, to the searching of the scriptures, to humiliation of soul and confession of sin.

There is a veil that separates the spiritual world from the natural world. We, as carnal beings see with the natural eyes, but at times, we see with the eyes of the heart with spiritual vision. It is during these times that God gives us glimpses of our marvelous future. He may even show us dangers lurking and waiting to manifest so that we can pray and cast them down. Oh, but could that veil which separates the visible from the invisible be swept back and the children of God could see the angel recording every word and deed which they must meet again in the judgment, how many words that are daily spoken would remain unspoken and how many evil deeds would remain undone? God will bring to light the hidden things of darkness and will make manifest the councils of the heart (1 Corinthians 4:5).

The Book of Remembrance

A Book of Remembrance is written before God, in which are recorded the good deeds of *them that feared the Lord and that thought upon His name (Malachi 3:16)*. Your words of faith, your prayers of supplication and intercession, the tears of your heart and your acts of love are all registered in heaven. Your praises and worship to God, the diligent study of His Word and your kindness shown to His children are all registered in the Book of Remembrance. In this book, every deed of righteousness is immortalized. There, every temptation resisted, every evil overcome, every word of tender pity expressed, every act of sacrifice, every suffering and sorrow endured for Christ's sake, is recorded and faithfully chronicled in this book.

The Book of Record

There is a Book of Record which is being updated every day. As the Books of Record are opened in the judgment, the lives of all who have believed on Jesus come in review before God. If any have sins written on the books of record that have not been repented of, their names will be **blotted out** of the Book of Life, and the record of their good deeds will be erased from the book of God's remembrance. *"Whosoever has sinned against Me, him will I blot out of my book" (Exodus 32:33).* God has an exact record of every unjust account and every unfair dealing. He is not deceived by "appearances" of humility, piety and Godliness. He knows what's in the heart. He makes no mistakes in His judgment of character. Men may be deceived by those who are corrupt in heart, but God pierces all disguises and reads the inner life. If those who hide and excuse their faults could see how Satan rejoices over them, how he taunts Christ and the holy angels with their sinful actions, they would quickly confess their sins and put them away. Through defects in the character, Satan works to gain control of the whole mind, and he knows that if these defects are cherished, he will succeed in the end.

While Jesus is pleading for the subjects of His grace, Satan accuses them before God as transgressors. The great deceiver has made great effort to lead them into skepticism, doubt and disbelief. He has diligently tried to cause them to lose confidence in God, to separate themselves from God's love and to break His commandments. Now he points to the record of their lives, to the defects of their character, their contrast to Christ, which has dishonored their Redeemer, to all the sins he has tempted them to commit, and because of these he claims them as his subjects. Jesus does not excuse their sin, but shows their repentance and faith, and He claims forgiveness for them. He lifts His wounded hands before the Father and the holy angels, saying: *I know them by name. I have graven them on the palms of My hands.* Christ will clothe His faithful ones with His own righteousness, that He may present them to His Father *a glorious church, not having spot or wrinkle or any such thing.* Their names stand enrolled in the Book of Life and concerning them it is written: *They shall walk with Me in white: for they are worthy (Revelation 3:4).*

      This is why it is important to pray and repent daily. Even if you do not know of any blatant sins that you may have committed, simply ask God to forgive you of sins of omission, commission, negative disposition and/or negative thinking. As often as I can, I confess and repent because when I stand before God, I do not want any sins remaining on the books. I frequently ask the Lord to wash me from the inside out, search me and try me. If He finds anything in me that is not of Him, I ask Him to show them to me so that I can repent of them, and then I ask Him to lead me in the right direction. Surely, I find myself thinking wrongly, acting wrongly and saying the wrong things at times, but I quickly repent and try to get it right the next day. The searcher of wisdom will watch all their ways. This Christian walk is a daily walk and we must be vigilant of ourselves at all times.

The Book of Life
God's people shall be delivered, *"everyone that shall be found written in the book"* *(Daniel 12:1)* The Book of Life is the book that records the names of every person who will receive eternal life through the atoning blood of Jesus. To be blotted out of this book signifies eternal death. This book is similar to the Book of Remembrance in which are recorded the deeds of those who have

feared (reverenced) the Lord and walked in His ways. The same book is also called the Lamb's Book of Life because it contains the names of those who have been redeemed by the blood of the Lord Jesus. The Book of Life is referred to six times in the Book of Revelation. Those written in this book are saved at the Last Judgment. Yes, the Lamb who was slain from the foundation of the world has a book in which are written all those who have been redeemed by His sacrifice. They are the ones who will enter the Holy City, the New Jerusalem (Revelation 21:10) and who will live forever in heaven with God. Since the book of life is that which records all who have eternal life through the Lamb, it is clear that the Book of Life and the Lamb's Book of Life are one and the same.

TO THEM THAT OVERCOME

As Christians, the walk is not easy. In fact, Jesus plainly told us that we would have some tribulations, but God has equipped us with weapons to assist us on this journey, the fruits of the spirit, motivational gifts, spiritual gifts, the power of our spoken word, prayer, fasting, and reading the scriptures. In addition, He has encouraged us to also put on the whole Armor of God so that we can stand against the wiles of the devil. He has well-prepared us for the difficult journey here on earth and when we prevail, there are some marvelous blessings waiting for us. In the book of Revelation, Jesus outlines a few of the blessings that we will partake of just for being faithful and overcoming:

- *He that overcomes shall not be hurt of the second death (Revelation 2:11).*

- *To him that overcomes will I give to eat of the hidden manna, and will give him a white stone, and in the stone a new name written, which no man knows except he that receives it (Revelation 2:17).*

- *And he that overcomes, and keeps my works unto the end, to him will I give power over the nations (Revelation 2:26).*

- *He that overcomes, the same shall be clothed in white raiment; and I will not blot out his name out of the book of life, but I will confess his name before my Father, and before His angels (Revelation 3:5).*

- *To him that overcomes will I grant to sit with me in my throne even as I also overcame and am sat down with my father in His throne (Revelation 3:21).*

- *To him that overcomes will I give to eat of the tree of life, which is in the midst of the Paradise of God (Revelation 2:9).*

The scriptures above list just a few of the blessings that we will partake of by overcoming, so my words of encouragement are for you, as God's precious children, to be steadfast, unmovable and always abounding in the work of the Lord, forasmuch as you know that your labor is not in vain in the Lord. May the knowledge of wisdom be unto your soul. When you have found it, there will be a sure reward, and your expectation will not be cut off.

CHAPTER ENDING WISDOM KEYS

- ♦ Sometimes our own words and behaviors can cause problems for us. We often blame the devil for certain hell that breaks loose in our lives, but there are times when Satan has nothing to do with the problems we experience. He just takes the credit and has no problem doing so.

- ♦ You attract what you talk about. When you change your belief system in thought, words, and emotional pattern, you change your whole body, you change your situations and you change your reality.

- ♦ If your thoughts are negative, you will exude a negative disposition and the words that you speak will be negative, thus attracting negativity to you. If your thoughts are positive, then your conversation will be of a positive nature, thus attracting good to you.

- ♦ There is a veil that separates the spiritual world from the natural world. We, as carnal beings see with the natural eyes, but at times, we see with the eyes of the heart with spiritual vision. It is during these times that God gives us glimpses of our marvelous future.

- ♦ A Book of Remembrance is written before God, in which are recorded the good deeds of *"them that feared the Lord and that thought upon His name"* Malachi 3:16.

Epilogue

I had no intention on writing a book at this time, but very recently, the Holy Spirit spoke clearly to me and said, *"Write the book."* I knew that eventually I was going to write another book and I already had the title for it, but I had been procrastinating and had not started on it. However, I was obedient to the Holy Spirit and began writing as soon as the message was received. As I positioned myself to write each day, the Holy Spirit did the writing through me. There was so much being written that my mind was going faster than my fingers. Once I started, I continued until the book was complete. This book took me a total of 10 consecutive days to write; 12 hours a day for ten days, whereas most of by books would take anywhere from four to six months to write. This book was ready for publishing on day 13.

It is my prayer that this book has blessed you, elevated your spiritual insight and took you on a journey of enlightenment. It is the will of God that we grow up into Him in all things. As we develop spiritually, the stakes get higher, but the reward for overcoming is magnificent! God has already prepared us to be conquerors. He wants to use us mightily, but in order to get more out of God, we must give Him more out of us. He desires a more intimate relationship with us in mind, body and spirit. You are very precious to God and He delights in His relationship with you. By faith I want you to, *trust in the Lord with all your heart and lean not unto your own understanding. In all your ways, acknowledge Him and He will direct your paths (Proverbs 3:5).* May God answer all your prayers and reveal Himself to you in a way that will change your life forever!

If you would like to share your thoughts with me, please email me at merrittmia@yahoo.com. I would love to hear from you!

Love,

Your sister in Christ,

Mia

Dr. Mia Y. Merritt

www.miamerritt.com
merrittmia@yahoo.com
1-866-560-7652

Dr. Mia Y. Merritt was born and raised in Miami Florida and matriculated in the Miami-Dade County Public School System. She is an educator with over 18 years experience having worked as a teacher, Assistant Principal, College Professor and mentor. She is a Certified Keynote Speaker, Teen/Youth Facilitator, Prosperity Coach and Author.

Dr. Merritt has provided workshops, seminars and keynote speeches around the country to organizations such as the U.S. Department of Homeland Security, The Miami-Dade County City Mangers, Florida International University Executive Staff, University of Miami, Family Christian Association and many more.

She is also a Minister of the Gospel and is a member of Peace Missionary Baptist Church in Miami, Florida under the leadership of Rev. Dr. Tracy McCloud. Dr. Merritt is the recipient of the 2011 African American Achiever's Award sponsored by JM Family Enterprises, an award that recognizes impactful community leaders.

She holds a Bachelors Degree in Elementary Education, a Masters Degree in Exceptional Education, a Specialist Degree in Educational Leadership and a Doctorate Degree in Organizational Leadership.

Dr. Merritt is a published author of ten books on the subjects of spirituality, personal development, prosperity, self-empowerment, and adult education. Her books focus on living in peace with oneself and others by making right choices and understanding cause and effect. Her books focus on living with integrity and serving others. Dr. Merritt's challenges and experiences in life have produced in her the resilience, character and strength to persevere in spite of what challenges she face. She shares her experiences in order to inspire, encourage and remind that your past does not dictate your future.

www.ingramcontent.com/pod-product-compliance
Lightning Source LLC
Chambersburg PA
CBHW050643160426
43194CB00010B/1789